Natural Interiors

Natural Interiors

**Using natural materials and methods
to decorate your home**

Ali Hanan & Pip Norris

Universe

We could start with those who have championed natural interiors (Frank Lloyd Wright et al.), but the list would be endless. Instead, let's start with those behind this book. Without the guidance and inspiration of Muna Reyal, *Natural Interiors* would have never come together as seamlessly as it did. We'd also like to thank Liz Boyd for her nose for sniffing out naturally beautiful pictures (and thanks to the photographers too) and Lucy Gowans for her sensitive, elegant design eye. Thanks too to the rest of the Conran team, particularly Alison Wormleighton, the copyeditor, who all helped breathe life into this book. Last but not least, we would also like to thank our personal support team, Dizzy Gillespie and Andy Donaldson as well as our parents, Jim and Linda Norris and Elizabeth and Murray Hanan, who were the first to teach us to respect and treasure that fragile beauty, Mother Earth.

First published in the United States of America in 2001
by UNIVERSE PUBLISHING
A Division of Rizzoli International Publications Inc.
300 Park Ave South
New York, NY 10010

2001 2002 2003 2004 2005 / 1 9 8 7 6 5 4 3 2 1

Text copyright © Conran Octopus 2001
Design and layout © Conran Octopus 2001

Publishing Director: Lorraine Dickey
Senior Editor: Muna Reyal

Creative Director: Leslie Harrington
Designer: Lucy Gowans
Picture Researcher: Liz Boyd

Production Director: Zoe Fawcett
Senior Production Controller: Manjit Sihra
Americanization: Dawn Bossman, Elizabeth Smith

ISBN 0-7893-0668-9

Color origination by Sang Choy International, Singapore

Printed in Europe

Contents

introduction

Even in the most hardcore urban landscapes, nature sustains the human soul.

Just the sound of a fluttering breeze in the trees or the soliloquy of a lone dandelion in a pavement crack rejuvenates and replenishes the spirit.

Come holiday time, it's no wonder urbanites flee to spaces where nature reigns supreme. But nature is not just for the weekend. To find an inner equilibrium, we need to live close to nature. Our homes need to recreate the natural environments that liberate us. Natural, untouched, raw, wholesome interiors feed our craving, nurturing and nourishing the spirit. Artificial interiors, on the other hand, are the fast food of modern home life, providing a transient solution that leaves us hungry for more.

Natural homes are not a new concept: *Natural Interiors* pays homage to our ancestors. Our forebears fashioned buildings out of whatever was locally available: homes were hewn out of rock, crafted from trees, carved from ice and shaped from mud. We once lived close to the rhythms of the seasons, altering our living patterns to suit the environment. By living like this, the ecological footprint we left behind barely touched the earth. Once, the earth and its bounty were so revered, Native Americans even thought trees were poems the goddess earth had created for her lover, the sky.

Modern life is a far cry from our roots. Over the last two centuries, urbanization and industrialization have made nature a stranger. Surveys have shown that many of us now spend 90 per cent of our time cooped up indoors. In our high tech environments, we speak to electronic voices, not real ones; we communicate via computer rather than by talking; we work under the glare of fluorescent lights and inhale air that's stale or recycled over and over again.

It is no wonder that 'Sick Building Syndrome' – where inadequate, artificial environments have lead to ill health in workers – has become a twenty first century malaise. The adage 'you are what you eat' now needs to be 'you are how you live'. Inadequate lighting, toxic materials, stagnant air, ever increasing chemicals, and synthetic furnishings, all – over time – gnaw away at our health. And inadvertently, air starved, light deficient environments impact on our spirits too. Nature supports our souls and sustains our bodies.

Natural Interiors is a solution to a modern concern: our fragile environment. Natural homes are inextricably linked with the earth. Everything we do – as we have come to realize at our peril – has repercussions on the world we inhabit. When it comes to preserving nature's heritage home, gestures big and small

Left: *Sigeru Ban's Villa Kuru in Nagano, Japan, puts a whole new spin on the phrase 'open plan'. His beautiful home binds nature and architecture. Instead of painted or wallpapered walls, nature creates the background panorama. Air, normally imprisoned, is free to flow as it will. Sunlight, normally restricted by windows, streams in. Ban's villa is inspired by the ice cool modernists (think architect Mies van der Rohe), yet draws deep from the Japanese tradition of living with only the bare essentials.*

make a difference. When multiplied by hundreds, actions such as choosing sustainable, biodegradable products over synthetics and plastics and reducing the amount of toxic cleaners we use save our planet from rack and ruin.

Buildings that are timeless have a natural beauty. Architects have always used nature's tools – space and light – to build with. Some buildings, however, like those of Finnish architect Alvar Aalto, are odes to the light and warmth of the landscape. His organic, flowing architecture and furnishings pay tribute to Finland's fjords and forests. Another modernist, Luis Barragán, famed for his colorful Mexican-inspired designs, painted his buildings – inspired by wildlife, light and color – with only natural pigments. More recently, when the minimalist movement of the 1990s stripped down interiors to the bare essentials, the surfaces that were left were raw and natural.

Much of nature's staying power is derived from its simplicity (as the minimalists unveiled). Champion of natural materials, the architect Frank Lloyd Wright once said, 'Simplicity is not in itself an end nor is it a matter of the side of a barn, but rather an entity with a graceful beauty in its integrity . . . from which all that is meaningless has been eliminated. A wild flower is truly simple.' And yet natural materials also possess an inimitable beauty. Fads and fashions can change like the wind, but nature's 'look' endures. Natural charm and earthy looks transcend whimsy and look timelessly stylish, as the interiors of Frank Lloyd Wright testify.

Nature has also proved that her products are not only beautiful but also have a longevity beside which artificial materials pale. A wooden chair's patina becomes smoother and its color richer over the years. Unlike the human skin, time and use make a stone floor softer, smoother. Glass and metal are almost eternal, barely ageing at all. Textiles made of natural fabrics are resilient. And all of nature's materials breathe. Air flows in and out of a natural house like a tide, and it makes us breathe easy too.

In *Natural Interiors* we bring you naturally beautiful interiors and guide you through how to create them. We look at both the practical and inspirational elements of design and how to draw them together. The first chapter covers the elements of nature that our spirits seek: air, water, fire, space and, finally, light and color.

In the next chapter, we take a look at materials: what pragmatic nature has given us to use in our homes, such as wood, glass and metal, clay and plaster, stone and textiles. The third chapter advises on application – how to use these beautiful and practical materials in our interiors. Finally, the chapter on spaces looks at how to integrate the overall mix into a perfectly balanced whole, room by room. On pages 138–140, we've collected a source list of reliable suppliers to help you.

Take this book as a blueprint for natural living. It doesn't matter whether your style is urban chic, monochromatic minimalism or rustic simplicity – put the *Natural Interiors* ethos to work in your home. Your spirit will thank you.

Top and above: *Designed by Future Systems, this house was nicknamed the 'Teletubby House' after the bunker home in a children's TV series. On the Welsh coast of Britain, it is an exemplar of environmentally tuned-in architecture. The surrounding landscape is unaltered; the house sits unobtrusively within it. The turf roof, covered with fescue, a local fine-bladed grass, camouflages and insulates the house. Double glazed walls maximize light into the interior. Porthole windows, made from yacht fittings, allow cross ventilation.*

Elements

earth

Ever since we first sought shelter, humans have fashioned dwellings out of the earth.

From the beginning, we harnessed what we found – plants (wattle, cane, rush, trees), animal hides, rocks, stones, mud, clay, dung – to make our dwellings. We developed a detailed knowledge of these natural building materials out of necessity, as we had to ensure a roof over our heads. One of the most basic forms of shelter was the cave. And, oddly enough, throughout the world today some 40 million people, such as the inhabitants of Cappadocia, Turkey, still live in cave dwellings.

In today's world, as our interiors have become increasingly urbanized and sanitized, we have hankered for mother earth's calling card in our interiors. In preindustrial, prechemical days we developed an innate feel for how the earth's booty could be used, and in developing countries, as well as many other places, this tradition is still strong. From the egg-shaped, baked-earth houses of Dogon villages in Mali and the grass-thatched, circular earth dwellings of the Native Americans to the pinewood log cabins dotted around Finnish lakes, the earth remains an intrinsic part of the building and decorating process.

We still adhere to regional traditions of building and furnishing our homes. When the settlers pushed into America, they chopped down trees from the forests and built log cabins, based on Norse,

German and Scottish traditions. In Japanese houses, great attention is paid to ensuring that the materials come from the earth. The floors are laid with tatami mats, woven from fragrant rush, while the sliding screens are made from mulberry paper and cedarwood.

On another level, the eponymous earth itself has provided us with an intuitive building block. During the day buildings made of earth absorb the heat of the sun, and hem it in at night; in the winter earth buildings keep warm, and in summer they are a cool sanctuary. Modern architects still cherish its insulating properties: twentieth century Mexican architect Javier Senosian Aguilar's funky burrows,

Opposite: *Nature thoughtfully fashions her materials to cater to local environments. In Mali, Africa, the Dogon tribe constructs organically shaped homes from earth. Under the burning African sun, the thick earthen walls provide vital protection against intense heat during the day and then resonate with the absorbed warmth during the evening after the sun has disappeared.*

Right: *A fairy tale cabin in Norwegian woods. Like earth, wood regulates the indoor climate and 'breathes' – air passes through it. Grass on the roof adds an extra layer of natural insulation and waterproofing. In winter,* *cattle shelter on the ground floor (hence the wide opening), while humans live above. Warm air rises, so the heat from the cattle acts like underfloor heating. When you have cows, who needs radiators?*

tunnelled beneath Mexico City, were perfectly suited to Mexico's climes, while Norman Foster's Willis Faber Building in Ipswich, England (1975), was capped with a turf roof, which provided a blanket of earthy insulation.

Aside from using earth in its raw state to construct and insulate buildings, we have worked out how to utilize fired earth in the form of bricks, tiles and ceramics. The earth also produces other materials for us to use in our buildings, such as plants (timber, cane, grass, cotton, flax) and minerals. Things that come from the earth seem to blend together seamlessly: take limestone and slate, which come in shades of dark grey, green, red, purple and rust. Stone merges effortlessly with the many hues of wood, from chocolate brown and ruddy red to warm ochre and creamy white. It's almost as though mother earth planned her wardrobe that way.

Other cultures regard the element of earth as an essential not only for building solid homes but also for spiritual harmony. In feng shui – an ancient Chinese practice that has stormed into Western interior design philosophy – earth is associated with openness, balance, honesty and faith. The 'grounding' nature of the earth even surfaces in the English language: being 'down to earth', or having our 'feet on the ground' imply stability and security, qualities that are essential in a home.

There is something unnerving about an interior that lacks earth-based elements. Without some reference to the earth it feels lifeless, even soulless. Take ceramics – earthenware made by the

human hand somehow seems to have a soul of its own. The human spirit often finds the perfection of machine-made pieces artificial and lifeless; some of the allure of handmade ceramics is often in a container's tiny flaws, such as a fingerprint left on the inside of a coil pot.

On a larger scale, every design, decorating and purchasing decision we make impacts directly on our local and global environment. As the nineteenth-century American writer Henry David Thoreau once said, 'What's the use of a house if you don't have a decent planet to put it on?' Now more than ever, we need to consider this wider context and how our use of resources affects the benevolent earth itself.

Much of 'going green' at home is based around the four 'Rs': reduce, reuse, recycle and reject. From reducing our use of plastics and synthetics to recycling glass and paper to rejecting as much as possible products that are not sustainable, remember that gestures small and frequent literally make a world of difference. Make sure your interiors are 'down to earth' in every way.

Above: *While we in the West fill our windows with glass and swathe them in fabric, this window is filled with millet, which is held in place by a frame of millet stalks. The covering lets in air and slivers of light, but keeps out heat and prying eyes.*

Above: *If mother nature peered through the oval window into this game lodge in Makalali, South Africa, she would feel very much at home. The seat is crafted out of earth, the floor decorated with shell and the pouffe sewn from leather and stuffed with horsehair. The whole building is crowned with a wig of thatch.*

water

Below: *When we bathe, water soothes us. As the body becomes weightless, the mind is liberated. Alan Greenspan, one of the most powerful men in America, is reputed to spend two hours a day in his 'working bath' solving economic conundrums.*

Opposite: *New Zealand fashion designer Karen Walker creates a natural splash. Dive into the pool and you're surrounded by cool, blue water; come up for a breath and you bask under the sky; smell the forest and feel the breeze on your wet skin.*

Water is nature's gift to us.

Soothing, calming, healing and cleansing, water has for centuries been used in our dwellings as a tonic, a purifier and a healer.

Fluid, flowing H_2O has become intrinsically linked with our physical, spiritual and emotional lives, perhaps because it is so fundamental to our material existence. Our bodies are 66 per cent water – we can live without food for a month, but will die if we don't receive water in a week or less. We sweat at least one litre (quart) of water at night, and most of us don't drink the eight glasses of water a day prescribed to keep us healthy.

Because we live and die by water, societies and settlements have historically formed around rivers, springs, lakes, oases and wells – anywhere a source of abundant water was found, so too was life. Spas have been visited for their curative powers since the time of Cleopatra.

Where water has flowed, spiritual rituals have sprung up around it. From the bathing of the Hindus at dawn in the River Ganges to John's baptism of the first Christians in the River Jordan, water has been associated with notions of rebirth and regeneration. The Chinese even believe that water carries the essence of Chi, the source of life itself. According to the Rig Veda, the most ancient Hindu scripture, water has the power to give life, strength and purity. In Aboriginal culture, when the water spirit tried to follow its love, the sun mother, to the heavens but was unable to reach her, water fell back to earth, showering flowers, trees and grass with dew. In feng shui, water in the home is said to act as a powerful symbol of wealth and opportunity flowing into your life.

We thirst for water in our interior design, yet its importance had somehow been overlooked until recently. Bathrooms, once relegated to the smallest, darkest rooms in the house, are literally coming out of the closet – not only into lounges and bedrooms, but also back into gardens.

Bathrooms and sanitaryware are now so chic that they're no longer languishing behind locked doors or spoken about in euphemisms. We've grown to recognize bathrooms for the spiritual and physical sanctuaries which they truly can become. Françoise de Bonneville, in her *Book of the Bath*,

says that to 'plunge into water is to return, quite literally to the source of life and even – since psychoanalysis – to life in the womb'.

Now, finally, the interior design potential of water itself has been recognized, particularly because in these hectic times we increasingly benefit from its soothing properties. These are already familiar to those who reside in hot climates such as Spain where the home is generally built around a courtyard – a fountain at its heart, bringing with it a sense of cool and calm. And in Japan, the sound of running water has stilled jangled nerves for many generations.

Interior designers are now introducing water to create calming environments or an element of

surprise. Free-standing or wall-mounted fountains are one of the easiest ways of bringing water indoors and are slowly trickling into homes. The ancient practice of feng shui advocates placing them by an entrance way, so visitors instantly feel tranquil and refreshed the moment they hear the soft sounds of flowing water. Water rills, rather like moats, can act as a device to define an area. Set into the floor, they create watery demarcations that also reflect light and movement (these water systems recycle water through a pump, so the rill can be serene or flow gently). Still water is like a mirror set into the floor.

Outside in the garden, water features such as ponds, fountains, rills and streams have been

Opposite and above: *Two contrasts – on the left, the swirling outdoor jacuzzi pummels sore limbs and helps invigorate the body, while on the right, the tranquillity of this Japanese bath calms the mind. In Japan, bathing is connected as much with a pure mind as with a clean body. To refresh the spirit, the Japanese advocate bathing surrounded by nature. Here, the autumnal forest, the indirect sunlight, the granite bath and the wooden stool mean that the bather is as much immersed in nature as in water. A constant trickle of water in the corner of the bath soothes frayed nerves.*

around for centuries. The ancient Egyptians created formal pools decorated with lotuses; the Romans were famed for harnessing water to create lavish pools, baths and fountains, and in traditional Japanese gardens the element of water is ever-present, even if simply represented by a stone or kare sansui (flowing stone patterns).

The invention of plumbing in the late eighteenth century was an important innovation in domestic water use; finally it could run freely indoors. Over the last 20 years, however, the innovation has led to a steady increase in demand for this precious resource. Some reports predict that in the next two decades the amount of water we use will increase by almost a third. In North America, an average family of four uses up to 1,000 litres (220 imperial gallons or 275 U.S. gallons) a day – about twice the average consumption for a family in Europe.

Water is essential to our life on earth, so it seems crazy not to take this increased consumption very seriously – particularly when you consider that 97 percent of the earth's water is locked in seas and another 2 percent in ice caps, so that all we are left with is the remaining 1 percent. The United Nations predicts that during the next quarter of a century, wars will be fought over water. Even though that may not affect most readers of this book, the point is to use water carefully. Harness its healing, curative powers, but cherish it too.

Right: *Water is reemerging as a force in the interior design of contemporary homes. Here, a Japanese-inspired rill frames a dining area, adding peace and tranquillity to this urban London home. The towering leafy bamboo tree potted in pebbles exudes a quiet serenity like that found in woodlands and forests.*

fire

Fire appeals to an atavistic, primal instinct deep within us.

We originally used fire to clear land, to protect us, and to provide warmth, cook our food and heat our water. Fire was a tool, a weapon and a source of comfort, all rolled into one. The hearth was the fulcrum of family life. Whole families heated water and dunked themselves in large tubs by the fireside. In Victorian times, one's status was judged by the quality of fireside accessories. Bellows came decorated with elephant ivory, hearth sweepers had brush tips made of fine horsehair and stokers were of pure silver.

Cultures around the globe ignite fires to celebrate rites of passage: wherever there has been a ritual there has been a fire and a feast. The ancient tradition of feng shui maintains that every home needs this element. Fire, according to feng shui, brings with it activity and passion; without it, homes are lifeless and dull. In our domestic interiors, an open fireplace or stove is always the life and soul of the party. A good fire roars, spits and crackles.

The smoke produced by fires, however, consists of unburned carbon or soot, tar particles and hydrocarbons, renowned for creating dust and grime, and causing respiratory diseases. In 1952, London's worst smog lasted for several days and caused several thousand respiratory related deaths. As a result, domestic fires were snuffed out. Burning combustible fuel, such as wood and coal, was banned in urban areas. Aside from polluting the air outdoors, fires were also credited with damaging the indoor environment. Any draughty, clogged up or cracked chimneys meant that smoke was regurgitated back into living rooms.

Throughout the 1960s hearths were stripped out of homes. Fires became unfashionable till the 1970s, when gas and electric fires proliferated. These 'living flame' models, however, paled beside the real thing. One of the complaints about the then 'new' fires was that they lacked the heat of real fires. Yet, ironically, fires themselves are not heat efficient: only a tenth of the warmth goes back into the room.

So how do we appease our primal urge for flames and still have inviting, ecologically sound fires? A number of natural smokeless fuels are now on the market. Anthracite – dug from deep down in

the earth's strata and therefore a purer compound than household coal – is an ecologically 'clean', if expensive, fuel. Manufactured coals are also 'preburned' to eliminate smoke.

Gas fires have come a long way since their 'living flame' ancestors. The fireplace's most recent reincarnation has been as the 'hole in the wall' fire, the latest accessory for modernist and minimalist homes. A circular gas burner, placed under pebbles or logs, is ignited and controlled by remote control, creating flames that flicker and dance. It's clean and fuss free – there's no grate to sweep out or firewood to season.

The kind of fuel you can burn depends on where you live, so check local regulations. Even with the restrictions on wood fire emissions, it's still possible to enjoy the hiss and crackle of a wood fire by burning wood in a stove. High performance stoves now have advanced combustion systems called catalytic or secondary burners, which are designed to burn off solids produced by the original fire. The stoves have glass window fronts kept soot-free by a jet of cold air, so fireside dwellers can still be captivated by the firelight.

On a practical note, stoves are incredibly heat-efficient. Ceramic stoves have a heat output of 90 per cent and if used in conjunction with a back boiler can also provide hot water for the home as

Above left: *For a contemporary look, dispense with fusty ornate fireplaces. Clean, sleek lines frame this fire like a work of art. In the summer, an unused fireplace looks ashen and unkempt. Sweep it out and add life and verve with vases of flame-colored flowers.*
Left: *Flames, even small ones, draw people to them, promoting intimacy and interaction. Curl up with friends on a sheepskin hearthrug.*

well as a place to brew a pot of tea.

If the quest for hearth flames seems all too much, opt for something much simpler. Stand some candles – tall and small, fat and thin, single- and multi-wicked – in a grate. Light the wicks. Strew squashy cushions and soft cotton or wool rugs all around, and curl up with your loved ones. Pour a hot chocolate made with thick, dark, melted chocolate, and let the storytelling begin.

Below: *The hearth is the home's emotional heartland. And this curvaceous contemporary hearth, flanked by a pair of welcoming leather chairs, serves this purpose well. Gas fires, unlike the coal or wood type, make light work of a fire. When not in use, a discreet cover pulls down to create a sculptural fire surround.*

air

Below: *Sea air was prescribed as a cure all to harried London inhabitants in Victorian times. There is validity behind the claim: whereas positive ions (posions), thrown off by electrical equipment, make us irritable and tense, sea air is charged with negative ions (negions), which calm and placate the human spirit.*

For the human body and spirit, there's nothing more rejuvenating than inhaling and exhaling lungfuls of pure, fresh air.

Unlike food and water deprivation – which we can endure for days – oxygen deprivation lasting even for only a few minutes is fatal. Cells must have a constant supply of oxygen to function.

We take more than 23,000 breaths of air a day, and considering that most of us spend up to 90 per cent of our time indoors, 20,700 of these breaths are taken inside a building.

Often the air inside our homes is stale and stagnant. An American survey has revealed that – surprisingly – indoor air can be up to ten times more polluted than the air outside, particularly in urban cities. In fact, America's Environmental Protection Agency counts indoor air pollution among the five most urgent environmental problems facing the United States today. The main problem is that homes, old and new, are being made airtight to trap heat and energy, but at the same time these sealed buildings prevent toxins and pollutants from escaping. At one time, old buildings were so draughty that the air inside them would naturally

exchange every hour or so, but in modern homes ventilation takes almost six times longer, which means pollutants gather.

To combat indoor pollution, every house should be able to 'breathe'. Just as natural fibers allow our skin to 'breathe', so the house's 'skin' needs to be made of natural materials. Choose organic plaster, tiles and paints or natural wall coverings, to create walls that naturally ventilate (see page 58). And don't forget the tradition of 'airing'. Throw open windows and doors to let in fresh air; dry washing outside; and air mattresses, blankets, duvets and bedlinen to invite precious air inside the things we wear and live with.

In Victorian times, a trip to the seaside to 'get some air' was a curative prescribed by English doctors for all sorts of ailments. Another reason that sea air is such a restorative is that it is negatively charged. In other words, it is loaded with negative ions (negions), which make us feel calm and balanced. Ions – molecules in the air that are

positively or negatively charged – affect the way we feel. In outdoor air, there are from 1,000 to 2,000 ions per cubic meter (cubic yard), and the ratio of negions to posions is five to four. Think of what it's like before a storm. A surplus of positive ions in the atmosphere makes us tense and irritable. After a storm the air, charged with negative ions, feels somehow released. In parts of central Europe, when the foehn and mistral winds blow in a surfeit of positive ions, they are known to lead to an increase in crime. In the home, computers, televisions, electrical equipment and synthetic materials produce

Above: *Incense – made up of ground plants, woods, tree resins, seeds, leaves and evergreen bark – has been used by cultures throughout the world to purify the air and appease the gods. Indian incense incorporates elemi, benzoin, patchouli and sandalwood. The Japanese include cloves, cinnamon, camphor and anise in their incense, while Arabic cultures favor a light incense scented with myrrh and frankincense.*

positive ions. To counteract these, invest in an ionizer, which will equalize the charges in the atmosphere and create a neutral environment.

Air carries scent. When perfuming the air in your home, ensure you use nature's air fresheners. Artificial scents are a sinister imitation of the real thing. Most actually contain toxic chemicals, like phenol, naphthalene and limonene, so when you spray them into the air you are, in effect, doing the opposite of freshening it. To use perfumes (not poisons), draw upon natural scents. Add cardamom,

cinnamon, cloves or nutmeg to simmering water for spicy aromas – great for winter firesides. For floral, summery scents, purchase bouquets of fragrant flowers, such as roses, tiger lilies and freesias. Dried potpourri, sprinkled with essential oils, perfumes the air all year round. Create your own varieties with flowers like chamomile, roses, lavender or vanilla pods. For scents with a theraputic twist, burn pure essential aromatherapy oils. Choose from more than 300 varieties to uplift, rejuvenate or relax.

Opposite: As many of us spend time at work or school in indoor environments where the air is controlled and recycled, it makes sense to inhale fresh air at home. A floor-to-ceiling sliding door here is pulled back so the living room extends into the open air. In naturally furnished homes like this, air is free to circulate through furniture and fabrics.
Above: Scent is airborne so site your living quarters where nature's aromas come with the breeze, like this Tuscan veranda. When you're in tune with nature, just a sniff of air helps you forecast the weather and tell the time.

Or use an ancient air cleanser from the East —
incense, which can also enhance or create the
mood or atmosphere of the room. Another
alternative is Native American smudge sticks made
from bundles of sage or cedar.

Nature has provided a natural air filter that we
can use indoors: plants. Houseplants oxygenate the
air and soak up not only carbon dioxide but also
pollutants. One plant that absorbs chemical vapors
particularly well is the peace lily. It is particularly
good at dealing with alcohol (found in glue, paints,
carpets, varnishes), benzene (found in carpeting,
chipboard, adhesives) and formaldehyde (found in
MDF – medium density fibreboard – fabrics, floor
coverings, upholstery, supermarket bags). Tulips
remove such vapors as formaldehyde, xylene (from
computer screens, paints, wall coverings) and
ammonia. Other anti pollution superheroes include
gerbera daisies, spider plants, rubber plants,
Boston ferns, bamboo palms, English ivy and
weeping figs.

Use houseplants liberally, particularly in
corners, where air becomes trapped. And, wherever
possible, let sweet, fresh air waft in.

Above: *To increase airflow, create doors that extend all the way to the ceiling, and generously proportioned windows. For the most effective cross ventilation, windows should be positioned opposite one another to help stagnant air migrate.*

Below: *Indulge in refreshing air by creating an alfresco living room. Even if you have only a windowsill, you can create somewhere to perch and breathe deeply.*

Above: *For a natural air filter, try the energy efficient houseplant. Not only do they sponge up carbon dioxide and oxygenate the air, but some also effectively soak up toxins such as formaldehyde, xylene and ammonia. Aloe vera (Aloe barbadensis) is unusual in that it is active at night rather than during the day, so is perfect for the bedside.*

space

Below: *Rather than being constrained by the architecture you have inherited, such as a series of rooms that are too tiny for anything, take control and create a bespoke home, adapting your space to suit your needs. Marry rooms in which the activities are related rather than separating them with walls. Sleeping and bathing spaces are natural partners, as seen in this chic loft apartment.*

Space is the element of nature we most covet.

Nothing liberates our spirits more than a seascape horizon or an infinite, endless sky. Wide open expanses give us a sense of time and perspective.

Yet, at the same time, we also yearn for a safe haven. We hanker for intimate spaces that make us feel cosseted and protected. We need private spaces in which to dream and to think. In our homes, the spaces have to be harmoniously balanced: we need open, inter-active spaces but also our own quiet dens.

How do we strike this balance? As Winston Churchill once said, 'We shape our buildings, thereafter they shape us.' In other words, we need to sculpt our homes around our lives, otherwise our interiors will dictate how we live. Traditional building layouts – along with the lifestyles they were once created for – may no longer be relevant for modern life.

The formal dining room, for example, is practically extinct. Contemporary life demands informality over protocol. The starchy, straight laced dining room was often only used for special occasions, remaining empty the rest of the time. Conviviality is now, thankfully, prized above etiquette.

Instead of separate rooms for each activity, kitchens, living rooms, dining rooms, bedrooms, bathrooms and hallways are now partitioned into related areas. Cooking and eating spaces or eating and living spaces are rolled into one generously sized area instead of two pint-sized rooms. Another room combination is bathrooms and bedrooms. After washing in a bath or shower we dress, so walk-in wardrobes and bedrooms are now married with bathrooms, separated by no more than a screen. Corridors and hallways, formerly often dark, forbidding places, are also being swallowed up by bigger, brighter spaces.

Luxuriously large spaces feel indulgent and liberating. To make a room seem wider, create horizons by having windows enlarged or installing skylights. Ensure views aren't obscured. Internal vistas – such as windows in inside walls – have a similar effect. Within these open spaces, hideaways are still needed, so don't forget to demarcate an area, whether by a hanging curtain, a sliding door or simply a visual reminder.

For most urbanites, space is often elusive. Real-

Above: *Light creates space. In architect Pierre Lombart's house in Johannesburg, South Africa, an arched ceiling surmounts rows of large windows that let in plenty of light, which is then reflected off the white walls. Traditional spatial rules of division are broken: the mezzanine bedroom crowns the main space, sharing with it the high ceiling.*

spearheaded by architects Claudio Silverstrin and John Pawson, inspired the clutter-free revolution. Achieving pared down, monastic spaces meant clearing away extraneous possessions. The space between objects, like silence between words, gained a new respect.

Most of us don't have the self discipline to live so sparingly (Pawson is renowned for having only three sets of clothing), and so making more space starts with having a place for the things you cherish. Create a home for everything and put everything in its home – then chuck out whatever is not needed. Do an annual spring clean of everything you have, taking stock of each item. Ask yourself: Do I really love it? Or would I rather have the space? Space should win every time.

Left: *A converted church in Belgium, now a family home, is luxuriously spacious, but manages through spatial trickery not to feel too lofty. A row of low hung pendant lights makes a visual connection between the ceiling and living area, creating a sense of intimacy so easily lost in large, public spaces. The dining and sitting areas are defined by furniture and lighting, with floor lamps designating a more private space in the sitting area.*

estate agents have developed a whole lexicon to avoid saying the word 'small' – such as 'bijou', 'compact' and 'cozy'. Yet, luckily, furniture manufacturers and designers are catering for petite homes and creating multifunctional, space-saving furniture, such as corner toilets and bidets, squat baths, foldaway beds and sofa beds, which means that those living in cramped spaces can make the most of what they have.

Creating a sense of space involves illusion. Stretch spaces by painting pale colors on all surfaces and use large mirrors with lights in front of them to reflect light around a room. Other ways of creating the illusion of space involve tricking the eye with proportion, such as using one piece of large furniture instead of many small pieces. Raising the height of a door in a low ceilinged room will also make a room appear larger.

Perhaps the most effective way of creating space is 'streamlining' or 'downsizing' – in other words, throwing out anything unnecessary. An entire industry has grown out of this late 1990s fad: 'dejunkers', for example, will come to your house and help sever your relationship with old letters, unwanted presents or other items that are past their use by date. The minimalist movement,

Right and below: *Large skylights crown a living room (right) and a bathroom (below) creating a feeling of space and a link with the outdoors. Anyone lying on the sofa or in the bath can watch drifting clouds during the day and view starlit skies at night. Skylights are an intelligent way of directing light into otherwise gloomy rooms.*

Opposite: *Blur the boundaries between outdoors and in, to create a seamless connection with nature. Just a glass pane separates the lounger from the outside world. The window also allows light to illuminate an otherwise dark ground-floor room. Staggered window slits on the upper storey will throw an intriguingly checkered pattern of light indoors.*

light and color

Below: *Let in light but not prying eyes with clever window coverings. A sheer curtain like this creates patterns with sunlight shaping dappled squares of light, yet still provides privacy. Other fabrics that are useful for filtering light include soft, smooth muslin, and rough linen.*

Light is our nourishment.

Without sunlight our bodies and psyches wither. Light keeps our internal clocks ticking in time to the earth's natural rhythms.

Our atavistic nature responds innately to light. Indeed, in many countries the law stipulates that rooms without windows are uninhabitable. An old Italian proverb declares that 'where the sun does not enter, there is a doctor'. Patients exposed to sunlight recover more quickly than those not exposed to it, while rats deprived of daylight fight incessantly. Light stimulates our metabolism and prompts our bodies to produce uplifting substances known as endorphins. If we don't get enough light, we are driven to distraction and despair.

Our inner rhythms are ruled by daylight. In the summer, our energy levels abound, while come winter we feel lethargic – we want to hibernate. This is because our bodies release a hormone, melatonin, which makes us sleepy when it gets dark. In the winter, when the sun is one tenth of its normal intensity, some people overproduce melatonin, leading to a form of depression known as Seasonal Affective Disorder, or SAD. Sufferers

combat the illness by perching in front of bulbs that emit 'daylight' rays for hours at a time. Most doctors say that exposure to at least six hours a day of natural daylight (including light coming through windows) is vital to our well being. So, for your health's sake, maximize the daylight you get in your home. Install skylights, enlarge or add new windows, create portholes or other openings – let in the light wherever you can.

Sunlight contains all the colors in the spectrum. Yet different colors influence mood and emotion in a variety of ways. What's more, different decades have very distinctive color palettes, reflecting social change and trends. The insipid blue and yellow palette of the 1950s paled into insignificance in the revolutionary 1960s beside the latter era's psychedelic reds, yellows, purples and pinks. 'Most people,' explained Verner Panton, a 1960s design maverick, 'spend their lives in dreary grey-beige conformity, mortally afraid of using color.'

Following the energy crisis of the 1970s, the prevalent palette moved into earthy browns, greens and oranges. In the 1980s, the 'decade of

Above: *Live in the light. Here the windows extend all the way from floor to ceiling, allowing sunshine to cascade in. Research has revealed that we need at least six hours of light a day for our overall well being, so site chairs well within reach of rays.*

Left: *Neutral colors are easy to live with. Here color and light are pitched against each other in a series of beautiful contrasts. Smooth, pure white sheets are juxtaposed with a roughly woven blue-grey bedspread. The white of the sheets is echoed in the bedside lighting, starkly contrasted with a dark blue wall.*

Below left: *Shadows are as important as color contrasts. As poet Jun'ichiro Tanizaki says, 'Were it not for shadows, there would be no beauty.'*

decadence', blacks, lavish reds and golds reigned supreme. And after the devastation of a stock market crash, 1990s society wiped the interior slate clean with spiritual whites and neutrals.

The color spirit of the present decade, however, may defy definition. Interiors have become chameleons as the prevailing fashionable colors

Opposite: *For inspirational colors, look outside your door; bring what you see back inside. Here the exterior leafy greenery is echoed indoors with a coat of fresh pistachio paint. A bowl of yellow lemons adds zest and brightness, while pink cushions inject verve and vitality.*

change with each season's catwalk parades. Today it may be aubergine combined with lime green, tomorrow violet and poppy red.

Defy the trends – let your own scheme show your true colors. To you, for example, red may mean passion, energy and love, but to another it might convey anger or aggression. It all depends on your experience of a color; whether you love powder blue because it was the color of your mother's favorite cardigan, or lavender because it reminds you of holidays in Provence.

Color is often associated with particular emotions. When we're angry, we 'see red'; we feel 'green with envy'; we 'get the blues'; and when we feel 'off color' we look pale. Use this link to create whatever mood you want in your home. Decorate with the appropriate color, adding toning shades for extra interest, and balancing it with one or two contrasting colors. Red, for example, marries with orange, purple and green, while blue is at home with green, purple and orange.

For inspiration, look at nature's color combinations. Spring's hues are fresh, with lime greens, cobalt blues and daffodil yellows. Summer's tones are washed out and hazy, with soft blues, verdant greens, pale pinks and lavenders. Autumn's predominant shades are gold, orange, brown and rust, while winter has the cool, neutral shades of grey, taupe, steel blue and cream. Pick the season that best reflects you.

Color and light work hand in hand. Dark colors absorb light, while pale ones reflect it. Small, uneven spaces are visually expanded when a pale, matt finish is applied to the walls. To make a cavernous, high-ceilinged room appear smaller, use a darker color on the ceiling, in order to draw it down visually; even a shade that is only slightly darker than the walls can have this effect. Decorate a small den-like room in dark, rich colors, and illuminate the room with soft lights and lamps.

Colors are easy to change with a coat of paint. If you tire of one shade, simply try another. Make light, however, your first priority. Shine with the sun.

Above: *Blue calms and soothes, which makes the perfect color for a bathroom – and in this case a bath, lined with tiny mosaic tiles. What colors mean to different people depends on their experience of it, however. To some, blue is aloof, cool and distant. Only you can choose the colors that influence your moods.*

Opposite: *Are you feeling stressed? Swathe your walls in blue and feel the stress dissipate. Are you lacking passion? Fire yourself up with red. Feeling unbalanced? Earth yourself with brown. Take a look at the colors opposite, find out which ones you're drawn to and then match the hues to your mood.*

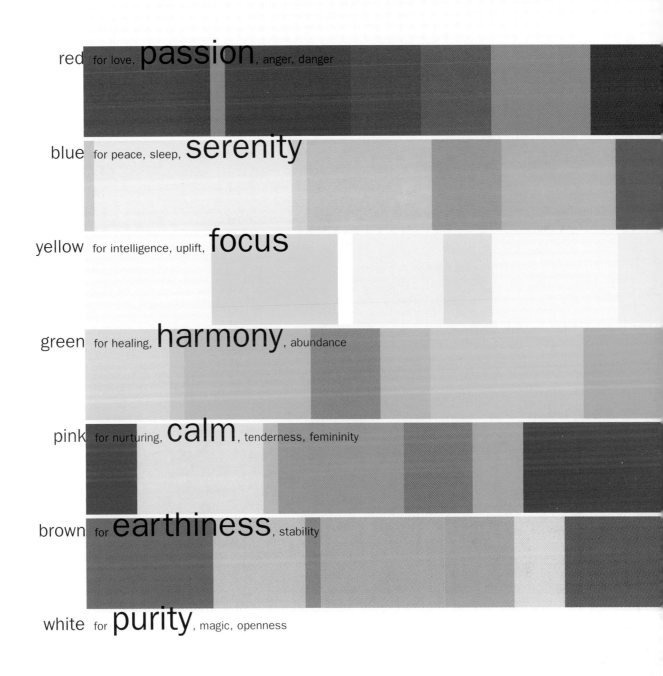

red for love, **passion**, anger, danger

blue for peace, sleep, **serenity**

yellow for intelligence, uplift, **focus**

green for healing, **harmony**, abundance

pink for nurturing, **calm**, tenderness, femininity

brown for **earthiness**, stability

white for **purity**, magic, openness

black for **mystery**, death, power

Materials

nature

Below: *The wonderful thing about nature is that we can easily relocate its essence within the four walls of our home. This artistic display of fronds demonstrates how the simplicity of nature can be turned into a sculptural display piece.*

Something is going on.

Gardening has never been more popular; neither have farmers' markets, yoga or aromatherapy. We want dirt on our vegetables, not shrink wrapping. We want natural not synthetic aromas to surround us. In short we want nature to impact on nearly every aspect of our daily lives.

A lot of this is subconscious. We're not thinking hard about it – it simply exists as an innate desire to get back to nature. For years, weekend hideaways, where we go to 'get away from it all', have invariably been connected with nature. When we are relaxing in this way we choose to connect with our natural surroundings – we take long walks in the bush, enjoy languorous swims in the sea, and sit in front of a fire drinking spiced wine.

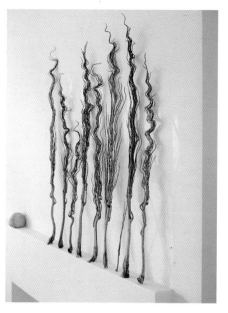

Our home environment has become of utmost importance – it needs to be a sanctuary, a place to escape the rigours of overcrowded public transport, constantly ringing phones and air-conditioned workplaces. Connecting with nature in our homes has become more important than ever because in so many aspects of our lives we are truly disconnected from it. The stale environments many of us frequent for eight hours or more a day don't satisfy us emotionally, physically or spiritually. In essence what we need to do is inject our personal environments with every piece of nature possible.

The simplest way of bringing nature into your home is with plants in their many forms. Running water over a fresh bunch of herbs such as lavender, or putting rose petals or essential oils into your bath, is a lovely way to lightly scent the water. Bring flowers indoors – nothing beats a fabulous vase of flowers, particularly if it has a wonderful scent. Use large leaves as bookmarks and napkin rings; arrange boulders as sculpture (inside and outside); put twigs into vases; hang chillies in the kitchen.

Arrange your garden so that scented plants, such as daphne, winter- and summer flowering jasmine, sweet peas, night scented stock, and the particularly fragrant wintersweet are somewhere that will enable you to appreciate them fully – beside the front door, under a window that gets opened often or along a path.

Try planting a chamomile lawn – its tiny leaves create a soft, luxurious outdoor carpet. As you walk, you gently crush the plant and release its aroma.

Above: *Houseplants add soul to a home. They need to be nurtured and in turn they nurture us by cleaning the air we breathe. Research conducted by NASA over the last 20 years has concluded that houseplants can improve indoor air quality – so do your health a favor and pot a plant.*

Creeping thyme is another star here: plant it between paving stones and savor the smell that is imparted as you brush past.

As mentioned in the previous chapter, houseplants are a must. Not only is their efficiency in replacing carbon dioxide with oxygen an asset that shouldn't be overlooked, but their role in absorbing indoor air pollutants is becoming more and more important. (Astonishingly, the chemical vapors they soak up seem to do the plants no harm.) Choose and position your houseplants creatively and they become an evolving piece of art, but think of them also as a medicinal tool, for that is what they truly are. Some plants are more effective than others at this – see the list on page 34. Aloe vera is a wonderful houseplant – sculptural and strong, it makes a bold statement. It also has well-documented healing qualities: snap off the tip of one of its leaves and smear the juice on minor burns or abrasions.

Plants are not the only form of nature we can bring into our homes – pets are warm, loving and living and are therapeutic in their own way. Anything that requires care and nurturing as pets do will add soul to your home and help to make it a relaxed, lived-in space.

Windows with views are a delightful way of framing nature and earmarking it for your pleasure, enabling you to claim it as your own, even if you don't have access to a garden. Open the windows and invite fresh air and the sounds of nature in as often as possible – you'll feel the benefits immediately. Keep your windows clean and your window dressing simple so you draw as much natural light into your home as possible; the purity of spring's dappled light playing gently on your walls is very hard to emulate any other way. As the great architect Louis I Kahn said, 'Natural light gives

Above left: *Natural light casts shadows that leave no doubt about the artistic merit of nature in the home. Combined with contemporary vessels, this display shows just how harmonious contemporary trends, nature and the home really are.*

Above center: *This earthy, yet contemporarily styled bedroom is so serene and fresh that there's a sense that a trickling stream must flow nearby. Lighting has been cleverly employed to highlight the pebbles lining the edges of the room, and the*

simple yet effective design of the alcove.

Above right: *Color is often enhanced and better appreciated against a stark white background. This has been used to great effect here to highlight the architectural symmetry of these single stem flowers.*

Opposite: *Create a show-stopper with a giant pane of glass and a cleverly planted foreground. Feature windows, especially those that don't open, are unashamedly saying, 'I am here not for humdrum reality but purely for your visual pleasure.'*

mood to space by the nuances of light in the time of the day and the seasons of the year.' (For more about light and color, see pages 40–45.)

Live in your outdoor space as opposed to looking at it. Eat there, laugh there, read there. Nothing is as close to the scent of summertime happiness as freshly cut grass, so spread rugs out on your newly mown lawn and lie on them. If it's not sunny, bundle up and delight in the feeling of communing with the weather.

Open your eyes and look around. You'll see nature's influence everywhere in modern interiors: pebbles are being used in flooring, twigs and fronds adorning walls and shelves while grasses and bamboo – formerly relegated to the outdoors – have come indoors in force. And remember, this isn't about adhering to a passing trend; it is fundamentally about creating an environment that makes us feel naturally at our best. A haven we need and a haven we shall have.

stone

Stone is a material that speaks of permanence, solidity and ancient times.

Much of the evidence we have of prehistoric life is quite simply a direct result of the enduring properties of stone. Images left carved in rock faces and tools fashioned from various types of stone are some of the strongest historical evidence we have.

The ancient wonders of the world – Stonehenge, the Great Wall of China, the Giant's Causeway, the Pyramids of Egypt and the lost city of Machu Picchu to name a few – are all inextricably linked with this material. In England the Romans and the Normans left behind an outstanding legacy of stone as a building material in monuments such as the 4.5 metre (15 foot) high Hadrian's Wall (built by the Romans between AD 122 and 128) and the Norman cathedral at Durham (begun in 1093).

With transportation techniques somewhat more cumbersome then than they are today, the only cost effective way to build with stone was to use that which was available locally. This meant that the English quickly developed distinctive regional styles. Old Cornish buildings were predominantly built in granite, Norfolk and Suffolk made great use of the locally available flint while the characteristic stone of the West Midlands was the English sandstone

known as 'New Red'. Often the stones are named after their localities. For instance, York stone is a sandstone from Yorkshire. This can also explain why such distinctive styles as New York's brownstone houses arose and why a country like Italy has used marble so extensively throughout its history – these materials were simply found locally.

It follows that locally available stone, apart from rising in an aesthetically comfortable way from the earth where it is found, will inevitably weather better in its own environment. Certain stones will crack, crumble or even shatter when exposed to weather conditions they are not used to, such as frost or prolonged damp. One of the most attractive aspects of stone as a natural decorating tool is that each piece of stone imparts its own unique qualities. The nature of its long formation within the bowels of the earth means that no two pieces will ever be the same – in these modern times of monotonous mass production, stone is still fiercely unique.

Granite, limestone, sandstone and marble are the predominant stones used in our interiors today and all come in a variety of colors. Granite is

Above: *The simplicity and solidity of stone are echoed in the proportions and lines of a trough-style sink.*

Top right: *Concrete is an incredibly durable surface and can be used to emulate solid stone.*

The beauty of concrete, however, is that it can be cast into whatever shape takes your fancy or suits your purpose. Waxing and buffing its surface will create an attractive soft sheen finish and also seal it against dust.

extremely dense and therefore very robust but it is getting harder and harder to source and as a result is becoming expensive. Most limestones and sandstones tend to be porous, so they need sealing to avoid staining. Colors range from creamy whites to nearly black, and the surface finish can be either honed or sanded. It is important to consider the use of a stone surface in order to decide on the finish. For example, highly polished granite would be unacceptable, even dangerous, on a floor but suited beautifully to a worktop.

Marble comes in an immense range of colors and is well suited to bathrooms, being impervious to water. Be careful, though, when wet it becomes extremely slippery. When decorating with marble, 'less is more', as it can look over-the-top. Perhaps this is because of the fact that stone looks best when used in its local environment. True marble is one of the few stones that England is deficient in – consequently perhaps, making it look at home in this context is a struggle. It's certainly hard to imagine it looking wrong in a bathroom in Rome. Marble is, however, a pastry chef's favorite.

From Marcel Breuer to John Pawson, architects have used stone to convey a certain sympathy with nature and to impart a feeling of solidity and permanence. We can build stone into our homes in quite simple ways – be it a marble basin, a granite worktop or a limestone floor. (See pages 90–92 for more detail on stone as a flooring material.)

Architectural salvage yards provide endless stone treasures and are an environmentally friendly way of purchasing this non-renewable resource. Because of its enduring nature there is plenty of reclaimed stone to be found. Don't expect it to be cheaper – it will, however, have a certain patina that only true age can impart.

Above: *When you are using such an aesthetically pleasing material as stone, you can truly let it take center stage. This sparsely decorated room does so and lets the floor sing to its own tune*

without accompaniment. Your eye is guided towards the floor because of the sharp contrast between it and the wall.

Above: *Reminiscent of the architect Frank Lloyd Wright's organic 1930s architecture, a dominant stone wall sits proudly in its modern setting. The slightly off center fireplace is a clever little quirk which adds to the playfulness of this extreme piece of detailing.*

tiles and plaster

Below: *Stair risers provide a great opportunity to create visual interest with decorative tiles. Mix colors and patterns to create a piece of artistry.*

Tiles are an age-old tradition.

The Louvre Museum in Paris holds glazed tiles from as early as the seventh century BC. There is no evidence of their use by the ancient Greeks or Romans though; it was the rise of Islam that first introduced them to architecture, where they were used extensively on both the interiors and exteriors of mosques. By the fifteenth century, Spain and Portugal had been exposed to North Africa's elaborate tilework and had embraced it with a passion.

Indeed, today when we think of tiles and their origins we often conjure up images of Spanish pueblos and the decorative tiling used so extensively there, or the classic blue on white style that is so distinctively Portuguese. But in actual fact, the process of baking clay has been around in many different forms for centuries. The finishes and end products vary greatly, despite the fact that they all begin in the same way, as earth, which is then treated and baked in a kiln.

Tiles are an integral piece of the history of their country of origin. In many instances they were made into murals, their patterns often harking back many

centuries. They have been used as decorative embellishments on the outside, inside, floors, walls – anywhere that there was a flat surface, tiles have been laid. Designs have ranged from small, geometric repeating patterns to large murals depicting historical scenes and stories.

The Victorians, once they had discovered the hygienic qualities of tiles, were quick to adopt them in their kitchens and bathrooms, butcher shops and hospitals. They particularly liked the small geometric variety.

The natural 'breathability' of baked clay, as well as its direct path from earth to our homes, is probably one reason we desire this material so much. Natural-colored tiles echoing the earth and its many shades, from terra cotta right through to cream, are a particularly successful way of harmoniously linking outdoor spaces with indoor ones.

Nowadays tiles are still used to a large degree in kitchens and bathrooms, though the weather in cold climates may deem them unsuitable for flooring in living areas. (Underfloor heating can,

Above: *Sometimes a home is lucky enough to have its own rustic history, as is demonstrated in this crumbling plaster wall. The old steel tap and display of vessels beneath seem to grow from their surroundings, so harmonious are they. Think long and hard before covering over such a surface with a crisp, new layer of plaster or paint.*

Left: *Bare plaster walls reflect natural light beautifully. With their warmth and tactility, they make a wonderful backdrop for virtually anything you care to place in front.*

however, help to combat this.) In hot climates, where the feeling of tiles underfoot is cool and sensuous, they are often used in every room.

Every real estate agent will tell you that kitchens and bathrooms are the two most important rooms when it comes to selling a home. People want to walk in and see both of these rooms looking fresh, hygienic and functional. Tiles come up trumps in all these aspects.

Tiles are a wonderful item to pick up on your travels. Buy some and use them to line a bathroom alcove or a mirror surround – or fix them to your stair risers for splashes of color and interest. They can be as subtle or as strong, as bright or as muted, as modern or as nostalgic as you wish.

Plastering has for centuries been used as a method in which to protect the exterior of buildings from the effects of the weather. The ancient Greeks and Romans even used plaster to waterproof their aqueducts and water storage cisterns.

Plaster was also the surface used for frescoes – murals painted in watercolors on plaster, the earliest surviving examples of which date back to 1750 BC. The finest frescoes were produced during the Renaissance in Italy about 600 years ago. The surface texture and thirsty nature of plaster are the very reason that these beautiful works of art survive today. The pigments used on the plaster were absorbed directly into it, a chemical reaction took place and the colors were sealed in, to shine vividly as an integral piece of the fresco for many centuries to come.

Lime plaster is the oldest of all the plasters. While it was originally employed as a material with which to protect exterior walls from the effects of the weather, it is now less commonly used than Portland cement on the exterior of our homes. Portland cement is far stronger and doesn't need the protection of washes or paints that other types of plaster do.

Bare plaster as a surface in our interiors is currently enjoying much popularity, probably as a direct result of a swing back to the textures and colours of nature. It is perhaps also in part because of the wonderful range of natural colors it produces, including soft whites, salmon pinks and tactile greys.

Plastered surfaces 'breathe' so they need to be treated accordingly. The traditional application of limewash or distemper is ideal here (see page 72), as is organic paint. Another idea, which Ilse Crawford recommends in *Sensual Home*, is to polish your plaster surfaces with beeswax, producing a delicate sheen.

In other words, leave plastered surfaces to their own devices, in terms of both aesthetics and practicalities. The texture speaks so strongly of nature and its unrefined beauty that a layer of solvent based paint on top would quite frankly be a slap in its face.

Plaster conveys an honesty that other surfaces strive to emulate – usually without much success – and is a wonderful backdrop for decorative fabrics, art and furniture.

Right: *Hard-wearing and attractive, tiles work well as a flooring material. The simplicity and solidity of this sink unit and bathroom furniture have left the owners of this home free to explore pattern with the tiled floor. Both the floor and the outside vista take powerful command of this striking bathroom.*

Right: *In this library, the shelving has been designed to draw attention to the raw surface of stone on the walls. The bottom shelf floats above the floor, enabling the shapes and textural contrasts of the stone and tiles to be appreciated.*

Above: *If you uncover a boarded up fireplace in your home, don't just think cast iron surround – think plaster and contemporary shapes. Good looking contemporary fireplaces can be easily styled with a smooth plaster surround.*

glass and metal

In today's world it is hard to imagine life without these two materials.

Just imagine . . . no more elegant glasses from which to sip Chardonnay, no stainless steel appliances, no windows to let light in and keep weather out, no brass taps or doorknobs, no mirrors to gaze into, no greenhouses to throw stones at, no wrought iron railings . . . In fact, the list of uses for these two raw materials is endless.

While both glass and metal come from relatively abundant natural resources, metals are nevertheless mined from non-renewable resources, and the process of manufacturing glass is very energy intensive. The recycling of both glass and aluminium results in a secondary product that displays virtually identical properties to the original. These recycled materials have therefore come to be used

extensively as a raw product. The positive benefit of this recycling is indisputable, as Anna Kruger points out in her book, *H is for ecoHome*. 'Recycling glass conserves both fuel and natural resources. For each ton of broken glass used, 135 liters [30 gallons] of oil are saved, plus 1.2 tons [2,600 pounds] of raw material.'

Glass was not really seen as an architectural material until around the mid seventeenth century. Progress in its manufacture meant that over time it became stronger (hence the ability to create larger panes) and clearer (therefore becoming something to be looked out of rather than at). This new-found clarity in glass revolutionized architecture and the way interiors were designed. Not just windows but entire houses clad in glass have stamped their mark on our architectural heritage over the last 50 years or so. An example of this is Philip Johnson's Glass House (1949) in New Canaan, Connecticut, which is totally transparent, apart from the bathroom – that is encased in a central cylinder.

Today a superb example of the powerful nature of glass as a material to be designed with is found at the chic Melbourne hotel, The Adelphi. Here a rooftop swimming pool eight stories up is cantilevered out 1.5 meters (5 feet), defying both gravity and common sense. What makes it particularly special is that it is glass-bottomed, so swimmers can gaze down on the street below.

Far left: *Apply your own frosted glass design by sandblasting or by etching with acid.* **Left:** *Old metal chairs stand testament to the enduring nature of this material.* **Above:** *This contemporary usc of mctal is a perfect example of how to apply it as a feature in your home. It looks good and will last much longer than carpet.*

Skylights are a good way to pour natural light into the deep recesses of the home, while glass shelving can enhance a room's feeling of space by lessening visual intrusion. A feature window – it doesn't necessarily have to open – can frame an attractive view, effectively bringing nature inside.

Frosted glass screens have become particularly popular, as they offer privacy and space delineation without the elimination of light. Glass bricks serve the same purpose but have the added advantage of significantly reducing sound. Much used in walls, both partial and full size, they are also effective as flooring where natural light is drawn up or down as a result. Glass staircases and landings are becoming popular for the same reason – the ability to maximize the natural light from above or below. (Advice and help with installation should most certainly be taken from an expert when installing or designing features such as these.) The nature of glass as a material means that it can be sandblasted (for a frosted look) and textured, allowing natural light play on it to great visual effect).

You will often see a large mirror placed above a mantelpiece – the mirror reflects and therefore multiplies any light that is already in a room. Use mirrors – large ones – outside too: they will move light around your garden, creating the illusion of more space. Set a few up in such a way that you can bounce the image of a particular flowering plant to within eyeshot of your kitchen window.

Metal is used in a surprising array of ways in our homes. We have embraced the good looking and durable stainless steel in our kitchens, not just for appliances but also for cookware, worktops, even flooring (although it can be rather noisy in this role). We are receptive to its cool feel, and aesthetically it makes the standard white appliance look somewhat like plastic. Stainless steel blends effectively with stone and sits agreeably atop tiles. We love the cool touch of brass when we open a door and the warm, rich, ruddy tones of copper.

The nature of metal as a material means that it can be molded, by skilled hands, into almost any shape that you desire. The Guggenheim Museum in Bilbao, Spain, is a stunning example of how metal can be successfully used on buildings as an exterior cladding.

In our gardens, wrought iron gates and fences are a familiar sight. In our bedrooms, metals are often used to great effect as bedheads. The

London-based designers Sharon Bowles and Edgar Linares have used metal to create some stunning interiors pieces. Their much-photographed free-standing lamp is made from many long, slim rods of metal fashioned into a fluid and strongly proportioned shape – something other materials would struggle to emulate with such ease.

Don't be afraid to commission works in metal. This is a fine way to realize a design that has been languishing at the back of your mind for years, and it won't necessarily be expensive.

Use metal as ornamentation, be it sleek and shiny or rusty and raw. Find pieces in a salvage yard and give them a new life. Turn scaffolding poles, for example, into towel rails. Take metal outdoors as well: its reflective qualities will bounce light around your garden, and it marries beautifully with water, enhancing the mirror effect.

Above: *Who said a nest of tables has to be old-fashioned and frumpy?*

Top left and right: *Frosted glass is a great tool for space delineation. Here a large pane has been used to partition off the kitchen from the dining area, ensuring that diners don't have to deal with the mechanics of meal preparation and yet are still able to interact with the cook. The fact that the partition is not full height aids this – voices float over and movement shows through while natural light flows unimpeded into the kitchen.*

plants and wood

We owe our existence on earth to the tree.

Trees play an important role in maintaining the soil structure of our land while also providing a natural habitat for many of earth's living species. The oxygen we breathe – our vital lifeblood – is a direct result of trees photosynthesizing.

Of course, other plant forms also fulfil these vital functions – earth's natural eider-down is stuffed with many different feathers!

Wood has long been respected as a versatile and enduring material for use in the home but, surprisingly perhaps, so have grasses and reeds. Thatched roofs, made from brushwood, straw or reeds, are integral to Britain's building history. Bamboo, which has been used for many years in Asia, is still much in use there, both as scaffolding and as a building material. Straw has been used for centuries as a binder in adobe bricks and as the main element in straw bale houses, a method that is enjoying a renaissance. So when we talk about

using plant-and timber-based materials in the home we could mean anything from pine and oak to rattan and bamboo, or even hemp.

Wood has been a ubiquitous part of furnishing, building and decorating a home for millennia. Many architects, such as the Finnish architect and designer Alvar Aalto, have particularly appreciated wood in a variety of guises. The inventor in 1932 of bent plywood furniture, Aalto had a feeling for wood like no other designer. The fact that he came from a forested place such as Finland helps to explain the important role that wood played in his groundbreaking architecture and furniture.

The use of wood in so many ways in the home, both inside and outside, demonstrates what a versatile material it is. Wood is used for wall cladding, flooring and roofing, tables and chairs; it is also found as toothpicks, cooking spoons, chopping boards and toilet seats, and is even used

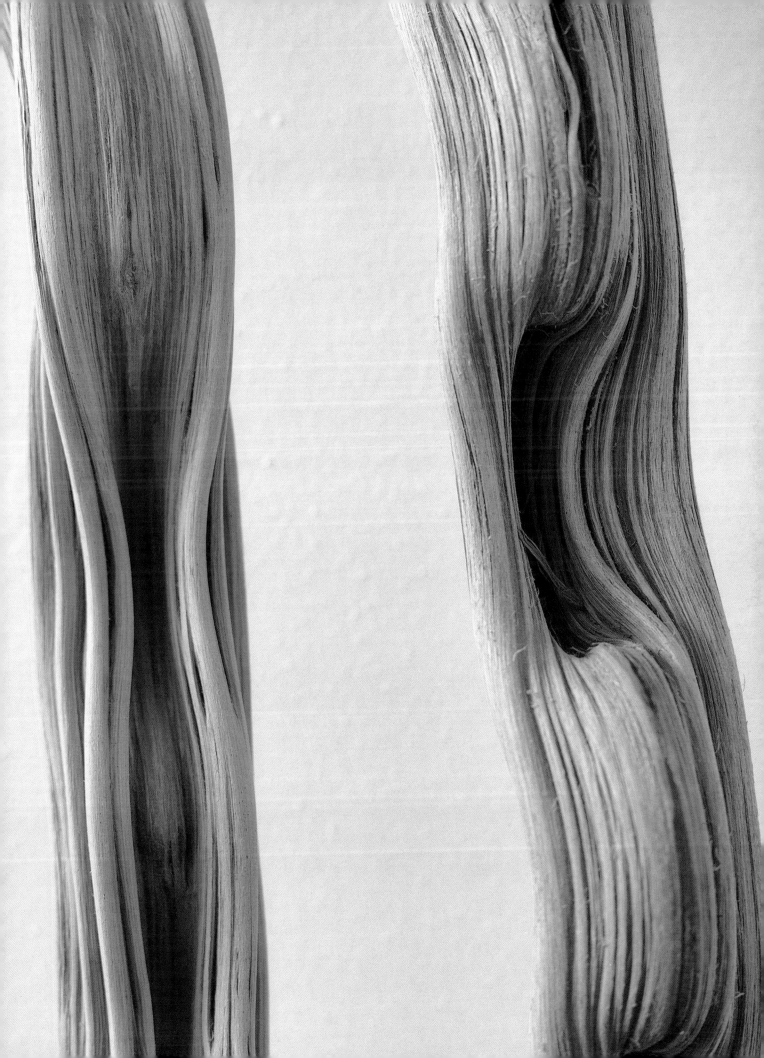

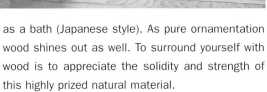

as a bath (Japanese style). As pure ornamentation wood shines out as well. To surround yourself with wood is to appreciate the solidity and strength of this highly prized natural material.

Plant fibres also come in many guises. Cane and rattan can be found as baskets and furniture, bamboo as furniture and flooring, reeds and grasses as thatch and flooring, and hemp as a textile (even the designer Calvin Klein has put hemp to use in his home collection). As all of these are drawn from a natural habitat, it is important to be aware of their fragility within that environment.

Wood itself falls into two different categories, hardwood and softwood. Generally speaking, softwoods grow faster than hardwoods. The hardwoods consequently have a closer grain (are denser) and are therefore more durable and less susceptible to

Left: *Simple and stark yet inviting, this room cleverly echoes the lines and shades of its blond wood coffee table in the design of the hearth. Both lend a minimalist, somewhat Scandinavian feel to this living space while the natural warmth of wood softens the clean lines.*
Above and opposite: *The raw beauty and versatility of plant fibres means that they sit well in many guises in the home. Here they are fashioned into a variety of pieces, from the decorative to the practical.*

disease and the effects of moisture. For obvious reasons hardwoods have in the past been highly desirable as a practical and beautiful building material for both the interiors and the exteriors of homes. Now, however, the ecological consequences of deforestation have forced us to consider more carefully the timbers we use.

The best approach to using timber in your home is to avoid all tropical hardwood. Unbridled deforestation has been destroying these tropical habitats

British mail-order company Twelve, Simon Turner, can trace the origin of the wood he uses directly back to the forest it was taken from, and is a regular reclamation yard forager.

Bamboo is extremely fast-growing, but you must still take care to buy it only from plantations that have been cultivated. The recent destruction of many natural plantations has caused worldwide concern for the panda, which relies heavily on a bamboo rich habitat.

for many years and the consequences are an ecological nightmare. Some of the most fragile species of wood are iroko, mahogany, teak, utile and ebony.

It follows that when we are choosing which wood to decorate or build our homes with, it is important to make conscious and informed decisions. Of the hardwoods, buy only European and North American varieties and ensure that these have come from a managed forest or have the Forest Stewardship Council (FSC) stamp of approval. Take similar care when sourcing softwoods, for as we move away from using the hardwoods, these too begin to risk deforestation. For more detailed information, seek out a copy of *The Good Wood Guide*.

One eco friendly way to buy wood is through salvage yards. In these places you should be able to find some beautiful old pieces with as much character as you could ever hope for. Seek out companies that are using wood responsibly (see pages 138–40). For example, the founder of the

All of these materials are highly desirable in the home – they can look as sophisticated or as simple as you like. And they will all sit as comfortably in a rustic setting as in an ultra modern one. They may require a certain amount of upkeep, like waxing, that synthetic materials will not, but this sort of interaction with the pieces that surround you helps to create a home with soul.

Above left: *Wooden flooring feels fantastic underfoot and is a true pleasure in a bathroom. However, while wood looks and feels fabulous, softwood will warp if it is exposed to a lot of steam or water.*
Above right: *The deliberate juxtaposition of woods in this organic living room* *strikes a clever balance between dark and light, sleek and rustic. Darkly stained walls provide a strong matte background against which art and flowers are strikingly displayed, while the shiny surface of the floor reflects and bounces light around the room.*

Above: *Echoes of a woodcutter's cottage are found in this warm and woody bathroom. The unusual and very distinctive wall cladding invites the touch as does the raw combination of a textured plaster wall with a large reclaimed wooden pole, a chunky slab of wood atop the storage drawers and a wicker basket. One gets the feeling that this room has been hewn from local materials and put together thoughtfully by the home's owner.*

paint

Below: *These bowls of earth-toned pigments found in a market in Morocco look as though they come straight from the earth.*
Opposite: *Be inspired by the colors of nature –* *there is certainly no lack of them. You'll never walk far in India without coming upon a colorful arrangement of powder cones, be they natural pigments for dying or an array of cooking spices.*

Paints in the home should sing to the same tune as materials used in its construction.

In *Natural Interiors*, stone, wood, earth and plaster are the favored materials. All are derived from nature and are loved not just for their looks but also for their texture and tactility. It follows that what we coat our walls, ceilings and woodwork with should have the same qualities.

Ecologically, paints derived from petrochemical components are bad news. Not simply the paint itself but also the disposal of solvents needed for thinning and cleaning pose a problem. 'Low-odor' paints are available but are still solvent-based and contain toxic ingredients – as, perhaps surprisingly, do 'water-based' paints. These, however, can be a good intermediary step.

Nowadays there are many naturally based options. They range from 'organic' (otherwise called 'natural') paints, which are made from non-toxic, plant-based ingredients including linseed oil, to the more traditional paint recipes such as distemper and limewash. These traditional applications were historically tinted with natural pigments derived from the earth (such as ochre), mineral deposits (for example, lapis lazuli, lead, malachite) and plants (such as saffron, indigo). Much trial and error went into the discovery of suitable pigments, particularly those that held their color and were easy to extract. One bizarre source was apparently Egyptian mummies: bits were removed and ground up, then, lo and behold, a brown pigment emerged.

There are many different methods of coloring paints today, including both natural and man-made pigments, either in powdered or liquid form. Alternatively, you may opt to buy your 'natural' paints ready mixed – remember that going 'natural' doesn't necessarily mean going back to the very beginning of all processes yourself. Look in the directory on pages 138–40 for paint specialists who can help provide you with the right advice and product, based on your specific requirements.

'Organic' paints may be a little more expensive than solvent- or water-based paints, and will also take a bit longer to dry, but they will significantly reduce damaging chemical pollutants in your indoor air. One instance where this extra effort and expense should certainly be deemed worthwhile is in the decoration of a nursery in preparation for a new baby, or the redecoration of a young child's bedroom or playroom.

Left: *A feature wall in a single block of colour can give a room an instant lift without adding any unnecessary fussiness.*

The traditional recipes of distemper and lime-wash have a big advantage over the solvent-based paints of yore, not just ecologically but aesthetically too – they produce an attractive soft and chalky texture, which is understated yet rich with character. Both limewash and distemper allow the wall underneath to continue 'breathing' so are particularly appropriate for use in old buildings, on new or old plaster and brickwork and on other porous surfaces such as Portland cement.

Limewash has been used for many centuries and in effect coats the surface being painted with a layer of lime, creating a wonderful chalky texture. It needs to be applied by professionals, as the mixture is slightly caustic (hence its antiseptic and insect repelling properties).

Bearing all this information in mind, remember that with a pot of paint and a paintbrush in your hands you can single handedly have a dramatic and highly satisfying impact on any number of rooms. It is the simplest way to stamp your mark on a home, be it modern or historic.

If you live in a period home, respect the era and try to emulate the methods of that time. If there is peeling or uneven paint hanging around on the walls, live with it for a while before you decide whether it is unappealing or not – sometimes a little time is needed for true appreciation.

Remember too that many visual effects can be created by utilizing color cleverly. For example a badly proportioned and uneven looking room can be visually ironed out by using the same color on all the surfaces: walls, ceilings, skirting boards and window frames. (See pages 40–45 for more about color and the surprisingly effective illusions you can create with it).

It is also important to take into account which way your room faces – does it get morning or evening sun? The paint color you apply becomes particularly important in a room that gets very little sun. With a little knowledge you can overcome this problem through the use of warm, rich tones.

Search the memory banks of your mind for colors that have appealed to you over the years. You'll probably find the same color recurring over and over – everyone has their own personal shade that uplifts them. Follow your instincts and seek out this color; don't settle for anything less than the exact shade. Finally, pay attention to texture, for this will add immeasurable beauty and depth to the surfaces in your home.

Opposite top: *Who needs art when you have paint? Play with color and paint finishes to create warm effects. Small slabs of color can be contrasted with a base color to add interest. Bring your walls into the foreground.*

Opposite bottom right and far right: *Respect the era of your home and choose its surface finishes accordingly. Traditional distemper and limewash recipes have been enjoying a renaissance and are especially appropriate for use in old buildings whose plaster walls need to 'breathe'. The matte finish and chalky bloom of a limewash or distemper finish will reflect light and bounce it softly around*

textiles

Below and opposite: *Fabrics, from the warmth of wool and the workaday nature of denim to the opulence of silk, can create a variety of atmospheres. Add texture and suggest moods with fabric. Metallized organza as shown opposite will add a sophisticated sheen to any setting.*

Since earliest times natural textiles such as cotton, linen, wool and silk have been used for both decorating and clothing.

Fabrics derived from flax are among the oldest known textiles while the method of silk fiber extraction from the cocoon of a silkworm was discovered as early as 1725 BC in China. It involved simply plunging a silkworm cocoon in boiling water, yet this largely unknown method of extraction was for centuries a closely guarded secret. The fabric woven from these fibres became so highly prized that by 300 BC it had become literally worth its weight in gold. Historically, the fibres from these natural fabrics were dyed with vegetable and plant-based dyes then woven into patterns, which, like tiles, conveyed historical scenes and messages.

Wool is another of the oldest fibres used by humans. It comes in many different guises, according to the animal fleece. It's an incredibly resilient fibre, even when wet, and so is widely used as a floor covering and as an upholstery fabric. Much of wool's beauty is in its diversity – it can be fine, fluffy or coarse depending on both the type of animal and the part of the animal's body it has been shorn from.

In countries with extreme weather conditions, textiles are still of the utmost importance. The cool, crisp nature of cotton and linen is crucial in a hot country such as India, for example, while the warmth of wool is a lifesaver high in the Nepalese Himalayas. Nowadays, in our centrally heated homes these features have become less important. It is still a good idea, however, to bear these natural qualities in mind when choosing fabrics, as subconsciously we feel more comfortable with a fiber that reflects the

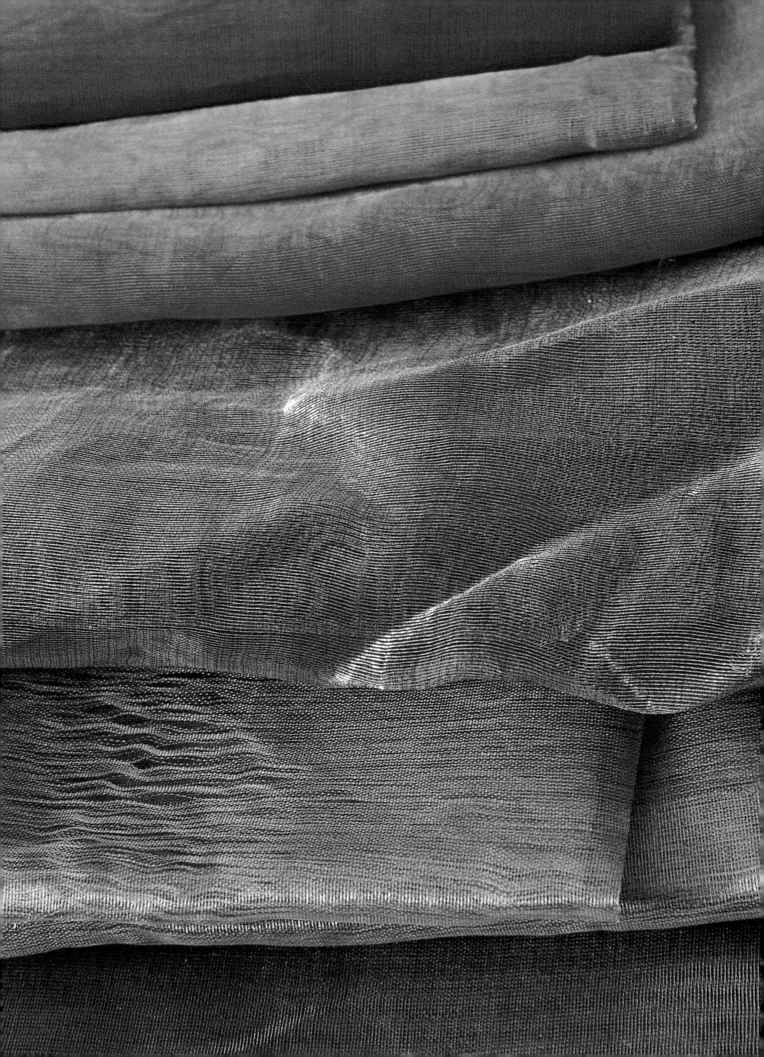

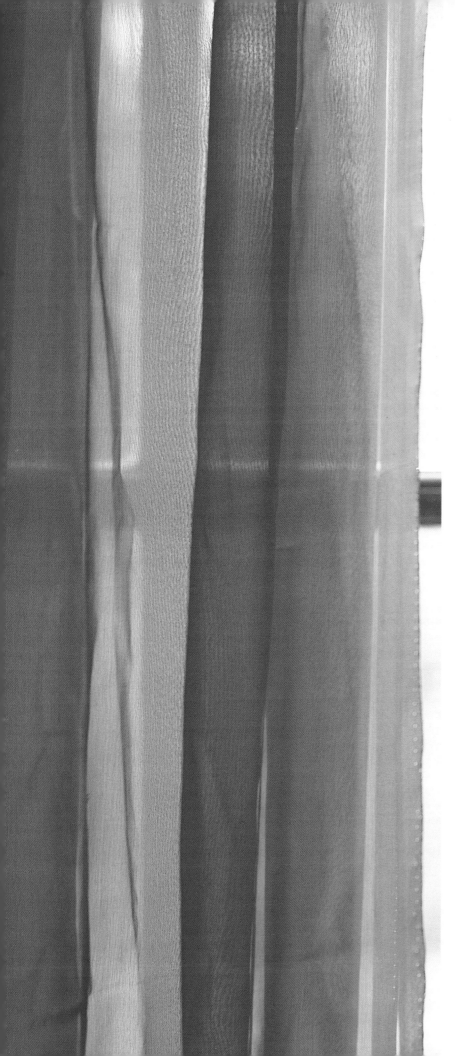

season. Think how reassuring a wool rug feels underfoot in the winter – it couples with the perfect hot chocolate – while in the summer months, a lightweight kilim atop a wooden floor pairs with a long, cool, refreshing drink. If we change the textiles we wear with each season, why not also change those that we interact with on a daily basis in our living spaces?

Don't neglect the qualities of durability, texture and weight – they all play a part in determining whether a textile is suited to a particular role. Sometimes your breath is taken away by the look of a fabric, but don't inspect it just with your eyes – touch it, rub it between your fingers, feel its texture. Use these criteria whenever you choose a fabric. With your eyes either open or closed, you'll find yourself drawn to natural fibres every time.

Textiles are employed in the home in so many ways. They are used for window and floor coverings, bedlinen, bath towels, table linen and upholstery; they are used to create beauty and aid function; they inspire and delight and are often the basis around which we decorate a room. A luxurious woollen throw can instantly transform the way a bedroom both looks and feels.

If you use natural fibres only once in your home, it should be on your bed. These fibres 'breathe', which helps to maintain your body temperature and facilitates a good night's sleep. A bag of lavender in the linen cupboard is a simple way of adding to the enjoyment of bedlinen; the aroma is delicious and is known to have a soporific effect.

Nothing beats the feeling of climbing into a bed of fresh, crisp cotton sheets. Egyptian cotton is considered to be the best quality, but do try to

Left: *Sheer fabrics across a window waft gently in the breeze and inject a wistful sense of summer into your home. Feel free to change your window coverings as you would your wardrobe – with the seasons.*

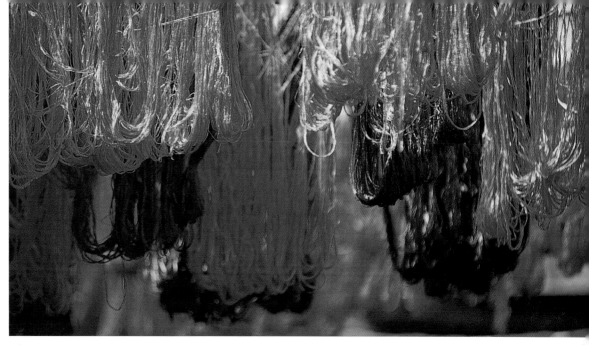

Right: *Silk brings an air of luxury and timeless beauty into the home. It can be dyed in vibrant colors, and its lustrous sheen captures the changes in natural light. The rich colors and textures of this fibre are captured here as it hangs casually yet elegantly in a Moroccan souk.*

Below right: *Nowhere are the colors and textures of fabric more evident and beautiful than in India: silks and cottons in rich pinks, turquoise blues and other vivid colors abound, as in these fabrics drying in the breeze at some bathing ghats on the banks of the Ganges.*

ensure that the cotton is labelled 'green' or 'organic'. This should ensure that they haven't been sprayed with formaldehyde for a wrinkle-free finish.

Bring crisp, cool linen into your home in as many ways as you can. It does require a lot of ironing, but nothing is quite so elegant as a table set with a white linen cloth and matching napkins. Exquisite vintage linens and trousseaux are found nowadays in many antiques shops and flea markets – a testimony to its durability.

Broaden the way you use fabrics – employ them in non-traditional ways and have some fun with them. At ethnic fabric stores, buy pieces such as silk saris or long panels of dyed muslin to use as colorful curtains. A length of beautiful fabric can be a piece of art: stretch it over a frame; hang it on a wall. Or string a light piece of muslin across an open window to enhance the pleasure when an invisible breeze enters your home: you will see its breath as well as sensing it.

Right: Throw textures and colors together in a melting pot to highlight their individual qualities. For example, nothing will draw out the visual texture of cool beige linen as well as a roughly woven, multicolored rug.

Left: *Vats of colored dye in Fez, Morocco. Many cultures still use traditional dyeing processes that are much kinder to the environment, and to our skins, than modern factory methods. Natural pigments derived from minerals or plants are preferred over synthetic, chemical dyes and often produce deeper, richer colors. As a general rule, the closer the color of a fabric to a shade found in nature, the more likely it is to have been dyed with natural dyes.*

Right: *Make sure the fabric you choose for each use in your home is durable and fitting for its role. Banish synthetics and wrap up warm in wool (top), sink softly into suede (center) and keep crisp and cool with cotton (bottom).*

Below left: *Natural, untreated fibres are of crucial importance for bedrooms, as we spend roughly a third of our lives there. Cotton sheets and wool blankets are the obvious choice for bedlinen, while linen or silk adds a note of luxury.*

Application

walls

Below: *Sometimes the best walls are the plainest ones – the ones that have been left alone to form a peaceful backdrop.*

Opposite: *Plaster is a wonderful surface with which to acknowledge bumps and curves and quirky alcoves, letting these become features and an integral part of the entire room's character, rather than a hidden horror. Do as the famous Spanish architect Antonio Gaudí did and grant your walls a freedom of form, which will enable them to look as though they have evolved directly from nature.*

Walls are the face of a home's interior.

Walls can be heavily made up or left *au naturel*; they can be the main feature of a room or can blend quietly into the background, leaving personal treasures and pieces of furniture to do all the talking.

Without the bounds of tradition insisting that we designate specific rooms for specific activities, walls have become a key structure and surface with which we can personalize a home. We can play with their physical presence in order to delineate spaces, creating either private cocoons or open, flowing, interactive areas.

When considering walls and how to address them as part of your decorating plan, there are several aspects to consider. In the initial stages it helps immensely to look at a floor plan – this is the best way to get a sense of your home's 'flow'. Examine it from this bird's eye perspective and ascertain how you want to interact in your home: decide which rooms need to flow into each other, and which rooms need to embrace privacy. Don't underestimate how greatly the removal or addition of walls will affect the character of particular areas of your home.

Note also on your floor plan the direction of your main sources of natural light and try not to cut directly across these, blanking out light. Thoughtful wall placement will enable you to maximize any natural light available and draw it deep into your home. Be aware that walls in many instances carry a lot of the building's weight. If you are about to remove a wall, employ a professional and ensure you are not taking down a supporting wall.

Walls offer an excellent opportunity to explore texture. The most beautiful walls are the ones we want to reach out and touch – those that have a texture that acts like a magnet. The material with which your walls are built will affect what can be applied to the surface. In some cases the material will have its own character, such as stone or wood, and recognizing the intrinsic beauty of this natural state is important.

Plaster walls thrill the fingertips and exude a warmth that no one can fail to be attracted to. With plaster we can exploit an uneven wall or enhance its irregularities by creating even more – anything from

Opposite: *Remember that your walls, floor, furniture and textiles need to work together to create a harmonious whole. Filled with a faded and carefree charm, this room has not one element of its decoration distracting from the complete whole. It looks as though it has always been just so.*

a silky smooth finish to a roughly trowelled one can be created. Ensure that any coating you choose to apply to a plaster wall is sympathetic to this material and respects its ability to 'breathe'.

Brick walls, rather unusually for a natural material, look good in either a raw or a painted state. Raw, they echo the land and earth from which they come. When they are painted, the texture continues to be exploited so that you don't in any way lose the sense of reassuring solidity a brick wall provides. (In addition, you can pretend that you are living in a Manhattan loft.)

Cladding a wall (or walls) in wood creates a warm and sensual space. The aromatic nature of many types of wood enhances this natural and very sensuous decorating option.

If you are working with plain plasterboard walls, enjoy the freedom this provides and think of your walls as blank canvases; be experimental and try

Above: *Be playful with your walls in an interactive area such as the kitchen or family room. Walls can easily handle the limelight as long as they are well maintained. Here blackboard paint has been applied to a wall, creating a surface that is fun, and useful, for children and adults alike.*

different applications. If using paint, choose carefully, making sure that the finish you desire will be provided by this particular one. Beautiful surface finishes can be achieved with the increasingly popular distemper or limewash.

Wallpaper has recently had a renaissance and this time around is providing us with a wealth of patterns and textures to choose from. Don't be bound by convention and assume you have to wallpaper the entire room. Wallpaper one wall and make a feature of it – this is the way to be bold with the pattern and color without drowning in it. Creating a feature wall like this with paint has become more and more popular as people realize how much fun they can have.

Right: *Covering an entire wall in eco-friendly tiles can be both practical and eye catching. The partial wall in this bathroom creates two distinct areas and an entirely waterproof surface to withstand splashes. When using tiles like this you must choose carefully and ensure that they do not come with an unglazed surface, which would stain easily.*

Above: *Often the inherent structure of a wall is a material in its own right, as in the case of a brick wall. If the structure is a wonderful natural material such as this, we should keep it as honest as possible. Sometimes, however, aging brick walls need a revamp, and here chalky white paint has been used to enhance the structure of this charming old wall. Its texture and original materials are still much in evidence.*

floors

Below: *The sophistication and warmth of a natural leather floor are difficult to beat. It absorbs sound, it is virtually unparalleled in warmth and resilience, and it looks oh so good. Each footstep adds to its character – as does the waxing and buffing process you will need to undertake as part of its maintenance schedule.*

Opposite: *Wooden floors will look good in any style of interior. And if you are combining the colors and grains of various types of wood in one space, you will always get a harmonious whole, never a clashing ensemble. That is the beauty of working with nature.*

Padding around barefoot at home is one of those wonderful after work pleasures.

With shoes and the stresses of work left at the front door, we can begin to feel calm and reconnected. The thousands of nerve endings in our feet mean that they are especially sensitive to their underfoot ally, so pay heed and do them a favor: cover your floor with natural materials.

With the vast array of options available today, you need to be well informed before going shopping. Ascertain exactly what role each area plays in your home and take note of the activities that will occur there – your flooring can then be perfectly matched.

Bathroom flooring will, of course, need to withstand steam and water without warping, lifting or becoming dangerously slippery. Children spend so much time on the floor (particularly if they cannot yet walk) that floors they use a lot need a considerable amount of yield and warmth. No baby will be happy spending time on a rough brick surface or a coarse piece of coir.

In a kitchen you need a hard-wearing, easy-to-clean surface; this too should withstand water and not get too slippery. The main priority for an eating area is that the floor be easy to clean. In a hall and living areas the floor's durability is important, but in a bedroom all you need is warmth and cosiness.

Over the past ten years natural floor coverings such as seagrass, coir, sisal and jute have become popular. Their natural good looks seem to fit into all environments, from sharp modern lofts to rustic country homes. Each is a natural fibre and its inherent qualities are a direct result of its origin. For instance, coir, made from the husk of the coconut, is rougher than, say, seagrass; however, it is relatively hard wearing. Jute comes from the stalks of the jute plant and is the softest, while sisal, although the most expensive, is also very hard-wearing yet relatively soft. The downside is that these coverings can be difficult to clean and prone to staining – seagrass, though somewhat rough underfoot, is the most stain-resistant. Carefully weigh up the advantages and disadvantages of these materials before you purchase.

While carpet comes in and out of fashion there is no denying that 100 per cent wool carpet is incredibly durable and has an unmatched natural resilience. According to the New Zealand Wool Board, 'New Zealand wool carpet rapidly absorbs common contaminants in indoor air like formaldehyde, nitrogen dioxide and sulphur dioxide, keeping the air free of many harmful pollutants.' They also

Left: *Sometimes rugged, sometimes sophisticated, stone is the darling of the flooring world. It is durable beyond belief and over the passage of time it develops a patina that stops you in your tracks.*
Opposite: *Bricks absorb and retain heat and so they make a wonderful material for using on floors. Bricks don't intimidate – we feel familiar with them as a material and feel relaxed in their rusty-red presence. Bricks marry beautifully with wood (think hearth and mantelpiece), sitting beautifully in a room that combines the two.*

say it has been estimated that 'wool carpets can continually purify indoor air for up to 30 years'. Clearly, wool carpet is not only durable, good-looking and soft underfoot, but it is eco-friendly too.

Linoleum conjures up images of tired hospital corridors but has come into its own over the last decade. It is a completely natural material, which has a certain amount of 'give' underfoot and has cleaning qualities that are highly desirable. Nor do you have to choose from the busy chocolate-brown designs of the 1980s – linoleum has had a contemporary makeover.

Wooden floors have a beauty that is a blend of the natural warmth of this material and its simple yet sophisticated good looks. Where possible, revive any wood floors you inherit: stripping, sanding and restoring the surface. If you haven't been lucky enough to inherit any, then head to reclamation yards, a fabulous way of obtaining wood with a past.

If you are laying new wood, take care which type you choose (see pages 66–8), ensuring you are not unwittingly destroying precious rainforests. Don't assume that this means you won't have much choice, though. Think of the shade you like and see if you can find a suitable wood that has a colour and grain to suit your home and your tastes. Be creative with wood, however, and use it in tandem with other materials. A combination of terracotta tiles and wooden beams, for instance, creates a stunning effect on the floor.

Stone offers a durable and undeniably elegant look. It is perfect for high traffic areas such as halls, kitchens or anywhere there is the regular treading of feet or the potential to track in mud and muck from outdoors or spill food. Stone ages gracefully, its appeal growing with every footstep. It works seamlessly when you want to blur the division between indoors and outdoors. A continuous use of

one material such as this will ensure that boundaries are fluid and the interaction between these two spaces will invariably increase. Underfloor heating has helped bring this and other hard flooring materials, such as clay tiles and bricks, out of the domain of warmer climes and into the homes of cooler countries. Slate is a popular stone that is very durable and offers a wonderful variety of colors, from the dark shades of bluish black to mossy greens and dusky pinks. Any porous stone surface will need sealing to prevent staining but the durability and simple beauty of this elemental material far outweighs the upkeep required.

If you live in a period home and already have the luxury of beautiful old floorboards in your rooms or wonderful flagstones in the hall, then treasure them. Another approach is to cover them with rugs and matting, which will define a space within a large room. Rugs are also a simple way of adding a non-permanent splash of color to any room to add uplift and contrast.

With flooring it pays to remember that cost-cutting will undoubtedly lead you to the less harmonious and less sensual non-natural materials. Because flooring takes the stresses and strains of daily life more than any other surface in the home, it doesn't pay to skimp.

Above left and right: *Define areas with rugs. They can be used to create a visual demarcation where previously a wall would have served this purpose. In large, 'swing-your-arms-around' spaces, rugs are helpful in defining cosy areas for reading or conversation. As an alternative to fabric, let mats made from natural plant fibres such as sisal, seagrass and coir add a natural feeling to a home.* **Opposite:** *Create a cool, minimalist look simply by using white paint on your wooden floors.*

furniture

Below: *Possibly nothing is as naturally magnetic in a home as a large, easy sofa next to a crackling open fire.*

Opposite: *The honesty and elemental warmth of a large, chunky piece of wood are unmistakable. Even better when it has been crafted into a well-proportioned occasional table.*

Historically the design of furniture has closely followed the architectural swings and rhythms of the day.

Architects often design furniture as a partner to the interior they've just completed. With *Natural Interiors* we need consciously to ignore transient trends and first and foremost consider the function required of our furniture and its all-important relationship with the human form. The aesthetics will easily follow if you choose natural materials and fabrics such as cotton, wood, cane, leather and linen.

In these hectic modern times we need to be welcomed into our home at the end of the day. Nothing is more inviting than a large, convivial table (a *Natural Interiors* essential), an oversized sofa or a good natured and comfortable chair.

Furniture fulfils many roles in the daily mechanics of a home. It has to provide storage and also somewhere to gather; it needs to create a resting place as well as a suitable area for entertaining. Aesthetically it needs to tie in with the decoration of your home. It must therefore reflect your respect for natural materials while still enabling the home to fulfil its practical function.

With the decline in available hardwoods, furniture made from natural wood veneers has become highly popular. However, it is possible to have a social conscience while still furnishing your home using solid pieces of wood and other natural materials such as rattan and metal, without resorting to veneers and plastics.

Inspire yourself at the beginning of a furniture hunt by heading to a salvage yard or to a flea market. Take with you measurements of the spaces that you want to fill. Nothing is more annoying than arriving home with a Victorian school cupboard as storage to find that it won't quite fit into the available space.

Try to support furniture designers out there who are environmentally conscious. Many of today's designers are creating cutting edge pieces of furniture using reclaimed materials. (See pages 138–40 for a directory of these.)

Create visual intrigue with one-off pieces of furniture: get a metalsmith or woodworker to produce a design you have hankered after for a long

time. Not only will you get a unique piece of furniture, but you will also be able to ensure that it is perfectly suited for your room or purpose. In any case, try not to clutter a room with lots of 'dinky' pieces of furniture. Even a small room looks better with only a few pieces of large furniture.

Try the furniture for size. This is particularly important when purchasing seating; you must sit on any chair or sofa you are considering and feel the support, or lack of it as the case may be.

Often furniture is needed for a dual purpose. For example, a large, comfortable sofa may need to seat three people at a time as well as allow you to stretch out on. Chairs might be needed for extra living room seating as well as enabling us to sit upright at the kitchen table or home office desk. Any furniture bought to be used for storage must be suitable for whatever is to be stored – it's all too tempting to allow the other role, be it seating, an extra worksurface or whatever, to take priority, at the expense of the less interesting function.

Also consider social events. A dining table must seat as many people as you envisage entertaining at a time. On the other hand, if you only occasionally entertain a large group but have room for a large table, it is still worth getting as you will undoubtedly use the extra surface. Or if you prefer a more informal atmosphere, make sure you have plenty of armchairs, floor cushions and pouffes for everyone to curl up on.

Whatever furniture you are buying, remember that if it doesn't fulfil its required function(s), it is bound to become a white elephant.

Create textural interest in your home with upholstery fabric. Choose cool, natural linens and cottons in the summer, and add warmth over the winter months with a loose woollen cover or felt cushions. For a relaxed approach to seating, pile cushions up at random.

Over time, natural materials gain in beauty what synthetic materials lose. A wooden chair will be rubbed smooth and age gracefully, whereas a plastic one will become scuffed and tatty. Enjoy the beauty of a worn leather chair; give an old wooden one a revamp, sanding it and oiling or waxing the wood – it's furniture's equivalent of a facial.

Remember that we interact with our furniture on an intimate level, so the material each piece derives from and the proportions that ensue from its design need in turn to nurture us.

Above left: *Sophistication doesn't necessarily suffer when natural materials are offered up in a somewhat raw manner, as shown in this convivial dining table. It manages to maintain a certain elegance despite its oversized chunkiness and solidity.*

Above right: *The soft 'come to me' texture of this throw and the curved glossiness of the bentwood chair create an opulent-looking combination. Experiment with juxtapositions of fabric and furniture, and enjoy the different moods you can create in this way.*

lighting

Natural light is intangible and chameleon-like, and it defies packaging.

Despite the changing nature of light, somehow the physical colors that are filtered into our homes with each passing season remain distinct. In the home therefore, the first rule of lighting should be to maximize the pleasure and health benefits inherent in natural light.

Since the invention of the incandescent electric light bulb in the late nineteenth century, we have for better or worse been able to emulate daylight in our homes. It therefore seems ironic that architects are now striving to come up with non-electrical innovations in lighting. For example, in redesigning the Reichstag in Berlin, Sir Norman Foster, one of Britain's leading architects made incredible use of the reflective nature of mirrors. Over 300 line the central inverted cone, flooding the building with an exhilarating amount of daylight.

When planning a domestic lighting scheme you should essentially be trying to emulate the subtleties of natural light itself. This is not as simple as it sounds when you consider that it comes in so many guises. In spring it is most delicious, dappled and mid-strength in its intensity. In summer the higher levels of light encourage laughter and an outdoor life. No sooner are we inside than we want to be outside. This is perhaps a good reason not to light your home too brightly at night. It needs to feel like night time and not a fake sort of daytime. In autumn the light is a completely different strength again. It is direct and strong but starting to fade in intensity and it enters our homes in several different ways, depending on the amount of leaves on the trees outdoors and the sun's lowering angle. In winter the light is often lacking that we simply want to get cosy and be cosseted.

There is always a defining day between seasons – a day when you say to yourself that 'it feels like summer today'. It is not just the change in temperature that triggers this thought but also the change in light. Take note of the light next time this feeling comes to you.

Possibly one of the best ways of emulating natural light in your home is to reflect it. Uplighting is an effective way to do this and will enable you to bathe a room in a softer, more natural level of light. Bounce it off the ceiling and back into the room. A ceiling will reflect light best if it is painted in a satin finish rather than matte. Reflected light will create

softer boundaries between the light and dark spaces in a room, so that the lighting feels more in tune with the changing shadows created over an entire day by the sun.

You can also help your lighting system to emulate natural light by choosing an appropriate bulb. The most commonly found bulb in homes is the tungsten-filament bulb, which casts a somewhat yellowish light. If you insist on using these, they are best if they have a silvered surface, which reflects the light up rather than directing it straight down in a monotonous beam. However, tungsten-halogen bulbs give off a light that is much closer to the reality of daylight; they are also smaller and therefore more discreet.

Compact fluorescent lamps (CFLs) have in recent years been gaining in popularity with their long life span and energy efficient qualities. As Rebecca Tanqueray states in her book *Eco Chic*, these CFLs 'use one quarter of the electricity of a standard incandescent light bulb and last for up to 13 times as long'.

Many people nowadays do away with harsh overhead lights altogether and simply use lamps. These offer great variation in a lighting scheme, and by using different lamps in combination you can create entirely different moods and atmospheres. Contemporary designers such as the British designers Sharon Bowles and Edgar Linares, and

Above left and above: *Fairy lights and tea lights twinkle in a captivating, night sky sort of way, encouraging romance.*
Left: *Incorporate nature in the light fittings. They will not date, will last longer and will sit more happily in your* Untouched *home.*

Michael Sodeau, are providing lucky modern day consumers with plenty of creative lamp designs to choose from. All produce floor lamps that entice and amuse in their celebration of light as a feature and of nature as a material. These lamps, among many others, are pieces of art in their own right, paying homage to nature as a material and as an inspiration for their organic shapes.

Don't forget to incorporate the romantic flicker of candlelight in your home's lighting scheme. Where our forebears relied on this for their light source, we now have the luxury of employing its subtle light simply to create a softer mood. There is nothing quite so pleasant as turning off the main

bathroom light and bathing by candlelight, the movement of the flame mirroring the gentle movements of your bathwater.

Nothing is so special as the purity of natural light. Enhancing this in your home should be your main priority and it can be achieved by actions as simple as cleaning your windows or placing a mirror carefully in order to catch and reflect the light around the room.

Above: *Every effort should be made to encourage natural light into your home. Privacy can still be achieved without sacrificing light, as is cleverly demonstrated here in architect Vincent van Duysen's sitting room.*

detail

Below and opposite: *As our lives and food become more processed, an inverse curve can be seen developing. We are garnering a growing admiration for and simple appreciation of the inherent beauty of nature's offerings. Flowers, foliage, berries and fruit plucked straight from the ground, vine or bush have some of the most appealing textures and shapes of all. Their natural integrity simply adds to their artistic merit.*

There is nothing so fascinating as the home that tantalizes our senses with curious treasures and objects.

Objects that we might not have thought beautiful – those we might not normally see inside the home and certainly wouldn't see in our local department store – suddenly bask in the glory of being chosen to star in our homes.

With the advent of central heating, microwave ovens and other time saving gadgets the need for nature in our homes on a practical level has lessened. It seems, however, that with this decline we are finding more ways of bringing nature in on an aesthetic level. Found objects (*objets trouvés*) are adopted as decoration in our homes far more laterally and creatively than ever before, as are beautiful pieces that have somehow, somewhere, caught our eye. Whatever it is, if it has been brought into our home on the premise that it delights us in some way, it will undoubtedly bring us pleasure forever more.

Try to display those things you find beautiful or meaningful in a way in which they, and they alone, can be appreciated. Arrange twigs in vases, bundle

them up and hang them as art pieces or weave them into small bowls to hold your jewelry. Display fruit and vegetables in such a way that their form and color can be fully appreciated: put lemons in a vase instead of flowers; place some green apples on a square white dish in front of a bright red wall. As Ilse Crawford states in her book *Sensual Home*, 'Creativity is left to artists, and taken out of the realm of every day. Bring it back into your life, even if it is only writing letters with pen and ink, or taking time to arrange fruit on a plate.'

Create your own piece of sculpture from a rusty piece of metal or a gnarled bit of wood – but do make sure that you are personally moved by it in some way. It should thrill you first and foremost – nothing looks so silly as an artificial attempt to create a 'look' for the sake of impressing others.

These details don't necessarily have to be enduring – run a bath and throw rose petals in simply for the transient beauty of it. Flowers are the

Above: *Your home is essentially a reflection of you and your tastes. Natural Interiors is about recognizing what inspires you and then bringing that into your home as a celebration of self.*

earth's way of laughing. As the writer Iris Murdoch once commented, 'People from a planet without flowers would think we must be mad with joy the whole time to have such things about us.' In many ways, they are the purest expression of joy.

All this collection and display may seem to go against the 'decluttering' grain – and, make no mistake, it can indeed be difficult to tread the fine line between clutter and the unfurling of personal

treasures and *objets trouvés* in your home. Be careful, therefore, not to suffocate your home, its flow or the people living within, for sensual pleasure will inevitably be lost if this occurs. Choose your displays carefully and there shouldn't be a problem.

In terms of decorating, the small details and decisions in your home are as important as the large ones. A house clad in beautiful timber with elemental stone as its flooring and honest plaster walls still has the ability to irritate if the details aren't right.

Above: *A slice of history always helps to ground our interior design. History creates a talking point: something to mull over, to amuse, to garner stories from. History helps to give a home soul.*

For example, entering a home through a lightweight door fitted with a flimsy handle will disappoint every time. The front door of a home should suggest security and privacy, but it should also welcome and bid farewell with sincerity.

You should also try to keep eras and themes consistent when decorating your home – window latches should be in harmony with the windows they grace as well as blending smoothly into the room itself. This is not to say that fixtures and fittings can't be changed, but they should be kept consistent. If you modernize one light switch, you should change them all. Or if you prefer old-fashioned brass switches, for example, try to find a complete set in a salvage yard.

Try above all to create a home that genuinely represents those living within it. Ensure that it is honest in its use of materials and that the accumulation of the treasures and pieces within, be they large or small, has been undertaken with candor.

Above left: *Somehow a pile of pebbles and shells is reminiscent of childhood, reminding us of a time when gathering up treasures was what you did on a walk. Children are in tune with nature and its simplest pleasures, from the squish of mud between their toes to the touch of a soft pussy willow bud against their cheek. Learn from them to rediscover these small, simple pleasures.*

Left: *Create bold statements with contrasts, coupling dark with light, curved with angular, matte with gloss. These contrasts in their polarity help us to better appreciate each beautiful and individual shape, colour and texture.*

Opposite: *When something is as elementally beautiful as this hand hewn vessel, you would do well simply to let it bask in its own splendid solitude.*

Spaces

cooking and eating spaces

Below: *Think of a kitchen as a creative workshop instead of as a place to process already processed food. Make natural food your raw material and cooking utensils your creative tools.*

Opposite: *Following seemingly endless health scares, we now revere and respect the honesty of organic, natural foods. Kitchens are reflecting this paradigm. Relish the wholesome virtues of homemade bread; the satisfying feel of well-designed cutlery; the integrity of pure white china; and the pleasure of sitting at a long, wooden table that extends a warm welcome to friends.*

The whole food experience, from purchase to preparation, is a time honored ritual.

The natural kitchen takes its cue from 'natural' food. It is primarily a celebration of natural living in every sense.

In Victorian times, kitchens were seen as unsavory places. The kitchen was the domain of servants, unruly children and olfactory offences, only trespassed upon when strictly necessary. Dining rooms, dripping with heirloom silver and linens, were status symbols; kitchens remained unseen and unheard. Today the rooms – and their hierarchy – have swapped roles as protocol has been replaced by informality. Kitchens are often said to be a home's greatest selling point, yet, ironically, despite being one of the most expensive rooms to overhaul, they are one of the first rooms a new owner rips out and redecorates. Modern kitchens have become status yardsticks.

On a practical level, kitchens are there to process food. Much of today's food, however, comes already processed and prepackaged, and as a result, many kitchens have been demoted to little more than fastfood outlets.

Natural kitchens, built out of natural materials, are places for earthy, visceral pleasure. A natural kitchen is a creative hub, not a laboratory. Instead of a battalion of microwaves, dishwashers, juicers, breadmakers and blenders, natural food involves chopping, stirring, whipping and tasting. It's a hands on, sensory experience.

The best food is home-grown and natural. As interior doyenne Ilse Crawford advises in *Sensual Home*, the recipe for good health does not rely on sell-by dates or on pre-packaged, pre-cooked and pre-loved victuals. 'Eat local, seasonal and familiar food rather than constantly searching for novelty,' she recommends. 'Relish the woody smell of mushrooms, proper bread, the piquancy of freshly ground salt and pepper. It's all about good quality plain food in perfect combinations. You barely need to cook!'

When revamping or building your kitchen and dining area, first look at the overall layout. While some revere the formality of a dining room with all its trappings, for others it's an inconvenience – the wall between the rooms creates an unnecessary

Above: *The formal dining room is an anachronism. Cooking and eating areas are now rolled into one large space, making the dining experience casual and convivial. Here the cook is able to chat to guests while the meal is prepared. And instead of traipsing down a hall and back again to serve food, the cook can take ready-to-roll meals out of the oven and put them straight onto the table.*

divide. There's nothing lonelier for a host than getting in a pickle over a hot stove while guests wait in another room. And while mealtimes are often when most households catch up on each other's news, the starchy atmosphere in a dining room is not always conducive to relaxed conversation. Taking down the dividing wall creates openness in every sense.

The floor in a kitchen is its foundation. It must be built to last and to withstand endless scouring, frequent spillages and constant battering. Sealed wood floorboards and stone fit the brief. Robust, hygienic and easy to clean, both have the qualities essential to a kitchen (for more, see pages 88–93).

If the kitchen is the heart of the home, the worktop is its main muscle. It must be easy to clean, waterproof, heatproof, stain-resistant and

Above: *This kitchen, right down to the storage, is a natural culinary paradise. Herbs, fresh and ready for the chop, thrive on the worktop. Tea towels and table linens breathe easy in wicker baskets. Downlighters illuminate the working area yet are not overpowering. A waist-height worktop means that the cook can work comfortably without stooping or stretching.*

Above: *Details count. Here the worktop is cast from robust, solid concrete, which looks smooth and seamless. Swivel taps enable allow easy use and feel good in the hand.* **Below left and right:** *Room with a view. A window over this generously proportioned kitchen sink (left) and over the food preparation area (right) throws natural light onto the task at hand. Use windows to inject life into otherwise shadowy areas.*

scratch resistant, and it needs to look good, too. Wood possesses all of these qualities. Close-grained tropical hardwoods have the additional natural advantages of being antibacterial and antifungal. If you are using tropical hardwoods, do ensure that the wood has come from a managed plantation. The main disadvantages of wood are that it soaks up water and will scorch. To avoid this, wipe off all spillages quickly and protect it from extremes of heat.

More resilient than wood, stone is also more expensive. For a durable work surface, non-porous stones such as limestone, slate and granite are best. Granite, formed from cooled magma far beneath the earth's crust, is the crème de la crème of work surfaces – it will look good for a lifetime. Whatever you choose, tailor your worktop to suit your height and ensure it's well lit.

Another large and important surface is the kitchen table. Tables provide a focus for a room and bring people together. Choose a big table, so that there is always plenty of room for others. Ensure that seating around the table encourages guests to linger. Offset hard edged benches with squabs, and soften chairs with cushions. Wood tops the table for favorite material – it's warm to the touch, congenial and inviting. Glass, while it looks sophisticated, is cold to naked skin; metal tables tend to have sharp edges and don't encourage guests to lean on the table with any comfort.

Ensure that there is ample space to store fresh produce. Build large, deep cupboards or a walk in pantry to provide storage space for pickles, preserves and reserves. Store basic vegetables like onions and potatoes in wicker baskets – the open weave of the wicker allows air to circulate through

Above left: *Naturally good for you. Crush fresh herbs, seeds and spices with a pestle and mortar made from hard wearing stone.*
Above center: *Dry dishes with pure linen tea towels, one of the few materials that is both moisture-resistant and stronger when wet.*
Above right: *Use fresh fruit and vegetables to decorate your kitchen as well as to flavor your food.*
Below: *A well thought out working kitchen. There's plenty of storage; a large preparation area; and an extractor fan to expel smoke and smells.*

the food and keep it fresh. Put some food on display: strings of garlic, bowls overfilled with fruits and jars of apricots and nuts instill a sense of plenty and ensure there is always something to eat at hand because a kitchen without food feels as bereft as a cone without ice cream.

One of the most crucial elements in a kitchen is light. Harness as much natural light as you can. Try to site the places you work, such as at the kitchen sink, to enjoy vistas and natural daylight (see pages 40–45). Position the breakfast area near a window too, preferably one that gets morning sunlight, to give you extra pep. Use artificial lighting to ensure all work surfaces are well illuminated – this will help to avoid cooking casualties. Buy full spectrum light bulbs to emulate natural light or buy incandescent or tungsten-filament bulbs to flatter food.

At dinnertime, always light candles. Choose candles in sensual colors – dining areas need stimulating tones. Red makes the heart race faster and whets the appetite, while orange or yellow sparks conversation.

Good ventilation is crucial in a kitchen. A hard-working extractor fan is a must above the stove. Refresh the air regularly by throwing open all doors and windows and keep a plant (see page 34) nearby to act as a filter. Tidy the rubbish area regularly.

Herbs can transform a meal from the ordinary to the extraordinary. For natural, flavorful food, grow your own herbs. Harvest regularly and freeze them to ensure that you will have a plentiful supply throughout the winter. Herbs will generally thrive on a sunny windowsill.

Pay attention to details. Natural accessories have stood the test of time and are still the choice of professionals. Cook using fine china, glass bowls, wooden spoons and steel saucepans. Meals seem to taste better if you cover the table with a linen cloth and eat with quality silverware off china plates. For some food, you can dispense with cutlery altogether and eat with your fingers, which children will love.

It would, of course, be inappropriate to clean a natural kitchen with toxic chemicals. Buy non-toxic, biodegradable cleaners or use basics such as borax, bicarbonate of soda, tea tree oil (a natural disinfectant), lemon juice, vinegar and baking soda. Start the natural ethos at surface level.

Above all, make the kitchen a sanctuary, somewhere you will enjoy spending time in. People receive nourishment not just from the food they eat but also from the company they share. Cherish food and eat it slowly, tasting each mouthful and enjoying it to the full. Eat, drink, talk and laugh.

Right: *A storage trolley on wheels makes easy work of serving up meals. This design, based on an old butcher's block, doubles as an extra cooking surface when needed. The apple-green shade, the colour of abundance and harmony, pays tribute to the world outside. A vase of poppy red flowers on the table instills life, nature and vitality.*

Right: *Salad sprouts, such as alfalfa (lucerne) and mung beans (Chinese beansprouts), in jars, will do well on the kitchen windowsill. All you need to do is rinse the seeds twice daily with clean water. Herbs such as flat-leafed parsley, chervil, basil, mint and chives will also thrive on a sunny windowsill.*

bathing spaces

Below: *The bathroom is one room in the house where we are free to be naked. Accessorize it with natural products to thrill your skin and fingertips. Wash your body with natural soaps made from vegetable oil; slough off dead skin cells with loofahs and natural brushes; and dry yourself with towels made from natural weaves, such as brushed cotton and linen.*

Opposite: *Architect John Pawson's bathroom design is so powerful that even just gazing at this picture instills a feeling of peace. Pawson believes that design achieves perfection when everything extraneous is stripped away; only what is either necessary or beautiful is left. Here, a rectangular bath becomes perfection. For complete peace of mind, there is no clutter.*

Slipping into the bath after a long day, you want your bathroom to breathe out too.

Bathrooms designed, furnished and washed down with natural, breathable, non-toxic materials create the perfect place for us to reconnect with nature and, most important of all, with ourselves.

The average person spends around three years of his or her life in the bath, yet when homes are designed or redecorated, the bathrooms have often been an afterthought. Slowly, however, as attitudes to sexuality have changed, so has our view of the bathroom. Now, instead of being condemned to the smallest, darkest room in the house – a hangover from the prudish Victorians – the bathroom is now the belle of the ball.

In other eras and cultures the bathroom has bathed in the limelight. In late eighteenth-century France, receiving visitors in one's hot tub was the height of fashion. But where once Marie Antoinette's mentor, the Abbé de Vermont, advised dignitaries from his tub, today's bathing rituals are a more intimate affair. In Japan, the Middle East and Scandinavia, communal bathing is still the

fulcrum of the community – friends and family go to gossip, read and relax as much as to bathe. For most, however, the bathroom is a place for repose and rejuvenation. If the kitchen is the heart of the home, the bathroom must be its navel.

When choosing a home for the bathroom, consider rearranging your present layout. Forgo the second bedroom, for example, and create a generously large bathroom instead. Or instead of an en suite bathroom, integrate a bathroom into a large bedroom or dressing room.

Choosing a bath is rather like selecting a bed: it's essential to try before you buy. When in the showroom, ask to hop in and lie in the tub for at least ten minutes. Check whether your neck feels supported, whether you can stretch your legs out and whether you like where the rails are positioned. If your bathroom is small or an odd shape, a round, triangular or square sit-up bath may fit in better than a conventional bath. Although porcelain has been the material of choice, there are

other natural options, such as stainless steel, glass and marble, which are all sensuous and stylish options. Wood too is beguiling. It retains the heat, smells aromatic when wet (particularly cedarwood) and is naturally antibacterial.

Most of us love the pick-me-up an invigorating dunk under a jet of water gives. Showers, now available as watertight units, can be fitted almost anywhere, such as under disused stairwells or even in hall cupboards. Prevent spray from soaking floors with a natural enclosure made from glass, or screen off the area with a concrete or tiled wall.

Accessorize with natural products, choosing bathroom accessories like wickerwork baskets, wooden duckboards and vegetable oil soaps.

Above: *Position windows to enable the bather to contemplate the world outside. Here a wide sash window bathes the bathroom in light. The bath, an old roll top model hoisted onto rectangular plinths, is given a modern twist. To keep the room clutter free, there's plenty of storage space deftly hidden behind the bath and lavatory.*

Natural products are also kind to the skin. Buy unbleached organic cotton and linen waffle towels, loofahs, pumice stones, and natural bristled brushes and store them in wickerwork containers or clay pots.

Bathrooms are most often used early in the morning or late in the day, so ensure that the windows will let in sunlight and air. Extend windows or punch out skylights if necessary. A smart solution for a boxed in room is a 'light tube' (a circular skylight with a highly reflective shaft), which will siphon bright daylight from upper levels into the windowless room. With regard to artificial lighting, opt for light bulbs with rosy, peachy tones to make skin tones seem to glow, and install dimmer switches to create mellow moods. Eyes need a break from artificial light, so try to utilize natural sunlight as much as possible, or light candles at night. Cover windows for privacy.

Instead of using harsh bleaches, try good ol' natural disinfectants. For a general cleaner mix a teaspoon each of baking soda and borax with two cups of hot water and one third of a cup of vinegar. Vinegar makes whiteware gleam, while a few drops of tangy tea tree oil mixed with a cup of warm water acts as a disinfectant. Mix in essential oil drops of thyme, lavender, pine, sage and rosemary too, as these plants also have powerful antibacterial properties – and they smell lovely. Or boil leaves and stems in water for half an hour (the longer, the stronger), strain, then use the water to clean.

The bathroom is the most humid room in the house, making it a perfect breeding ground for fungus and mildew. Prevention, in this case, is far better than playing Terminator with highly toxic removers. Using clay plaster (which absorbs moisture) for the ceiling and upper walls, regular cleaning, adequate ventilation and a humi-stat (a device that expels moist warm air when a bathroom reaches a certain humidity) will help keep fungal growths at bay.

Perfume the room with natural scents. The bath is the perfect place to harness the power of scent, so add six to twelve droplets of aromatic essential oil to bathwater. Alternatively, make a herbal infusion by gathering fresh herbs and hanging them in a muslin bag under the hot tap when you run the bath. Then dunk yourself. Pick scents that reflect your

Above: *Once we bathed in rivers, lakes and streams. An outdoor shower like this pays homage to our natural bathing past, allowing the bather to indulge in an invigorating dunk in the open air and sunshine. It's also very practical – as a way to slough off mud or sand.*

Top left: *Designers are using other natural materials aside from porcelain in bathroom design. Here a cast concrete basin, perfect for a small bathroom, exudes a touch of natural class.*

Top right: *A Japanese-style sit bath is an ideal solution for a pint-sized bathroom. This bath is tall enough to allow the water to cover the shoulders of the bather – what a perfect way to relax.*

Above left: *A wooden basin makes a beautiful and unusual alternative to ceramic. Taps are wall mounted to economize on space.*

Above right: *Natural beauty aids are more appealing than man made products. Volcanic pumice sloughs off dead skin cells, Epsom salts soften bathwater; and sea sponges (seen here) cleanse the body.*

Above: *A wooden bath (made from hardwood) is soft to the touch and exudes lovely earthy aromas when wet. Wood's other virtue is that it is surprisingly hygienic, being both antibacterial and antifungal. Here the bath integrates seamlessly into a bench-cum-bath design with storage at either end.*

Above left: *The Japanese believe in showering before a bath; to them, the Western tradition of just hopping into a bath is unthinkable. Here a shower positioned over a bathtub means that it's easy for bathers to wash first. The floor acts as a 'wet' area: water runs off into a corner drain.*
Above right: *A shower is tucked away into a corner, yet because it's encased in glass it doesn't seem to diminish the space.*
Left: *In UK fashion designer Karen Millen's bathroom, wood and concrete combine beautifully.*

needs: lavender, for example, is said to strengthen the immune system, relax and rejuvenate, while rosemary is said to be a tonic for frayed nerves, the circulatory system and the digestive system.

Ideally, your bathroom should be warm enough for you to roam around *au naturel*. Keep the temperature ambient: ideally about 77°F. Heat the bathroom with radiators, underfloor heating or coal burning stoves – don't rely on a heated towel rail alone.

Finally, always try to bathe with nature in view. A survey in Scandinavia found that patients in a hospital with a view onto a garden were twice as likely to recover as those with none. In traditional Japanese culture, a *furos* (or private bath) is always built where the bather can contemplate a small Zen garden. Bring in pot plants, stones, driftwood collected from walks on the beach, flowers, and turn bathtime into a moment to reflect on nature and all its beauty.

Above: *Although bathrooms are private spaces, sometimes they are also the ideal place to chat and catch up with loved ones. This rough, handsome recliner invites visitors and provides a place for post-bath beauty treatments. The bath, mounted on wooden blocks, looks like a sculpture. It's perfectly sited beneath a window, letting in fresh air and swathes of light. A nature-as-sculpture window display continues the organic theme and provides a little privacy by day.*

bedrooms

Remember when the bedroom was a sanctuary, a place to sleep and dream?

All too often in today's fast-paced 24/7 lifestyle, the bedroom is just another place to chat on the phone, watch television, send emails and work. As Terence Conran once said, 'It seems incongruous that the bedroom, which is by far the most personal room in the house, is also the most neglected.'

Perhaps it's because sleep itself has been sidelined. On average, we get 90 minutes' less sleep than our great-grandparents did. Before the advent of the light bulb just over a century ago, the average amount of sleep that was consi-

dered essential for good health was nine hours. Now the 'normal' amount has been pruned back to seven and a half hours. History has recorded some notable exceptions to these 'normal' sleep requirements, however: Leonardo da Vinci famously slept for 15 minutes every four hours, while Napoleon, Winston Churchill and Margaret Thatcher thrived on three to four hours' sleep a night yet still managed to run empires and fight wars.

In Napoleon's day, nocturnal privacy was unheard of. In eighteenth-century France, bedroom parties were all the rage. The boudoir was the 'in' place to receive friends, play games and gossip. Curtains were draped around four poster beds, to ward off draughts, not people. In peasant houses, siblings and spouses would bunk down together, often on straw mattresses, hence the expression 'hitting the hay'. 'Sleeping together' was about warmth and security rather than sex.

If sleep is so vital to us – and we spend a third of our lives indulging in it – then bedrooms should be put on a priority pedestal. Natural bedrooms help us reconnect with our own circadian rhythms, or 24-hour clock, an inheritance we've neglected at our emotional and physical peril. Bedrooms should also be strictly for sleeping, a place where the stresses of daily life don't intrude. As designer and architect Ettore Sottsass once said, 'I believe that everything in one's house should be comfortable, but one's bedroom must be more than comfortable, it must be intimate.'

When you're first putting together the jigsaw of your room layout, ensure that you site the bedroom in the quietest room of the house. 'Tell me something I don't know,' you may be saying, but all too

often it's the obvious that is overlooked when it comes to our sleeping dens. Avoid locating bedrooms next to noisy bathrooms or the kitchen, or facing a busy main road. If that's impossible, splash out and have your windows double glazed to cull excess noise.

Sunlight alerts our internal alarm clock and assists us with waking. Allow the sun to be your morning pick-me-up by positioning your room or a window somewhere so light can stream in. To let light in but keep prying eyes out, use sandblasted glass, a screen or a translucent curtain or blind in a fabric like lace or muslin.

Natural light might wake us, but as we don't usually go to bed with the sun, we rely on artificial light at night. A bedside lamp or wall-mounted light is essential for bedtime reading. Switches or cords within reach prevent cold, perilous dashes across the room at night. A dimmable bedside light, fairy lights or candles will help to create an atmosphere for romance. Additionally, rooms need well placed bright light, particularly if the bedroom doubles as a dressing room.

A bedroom without a decent bed is like a bathroom without a bath. A good bed is absolutely fundamental to good sleep – it's the most important

Left: *Beds don't necessarily have to be on bases, as this low level, Japanese-style bed shows. A well-sprung, supportive mattress is paramount, however. Plants, which act as natural air filters, are a must for cleansing and oxygenating the air in the bedroom.*

Above: *Gnarled wood makes a sculptural backdrop for this large, pristine white bed. The wooden floor below continues the theme, pitching the smooth and planed against the rough bedhead. Wood makes the perfect companion to the soles of naked feet.*

piece of furniture you'll ever buy. Oddly, we'll happily spend a fortune on a designer fridge and then scrimp on a mattress (perhaps because a bed is less 'on show' than, say, a sofa).

Yet bad beds can lead to back and postural problems, and are frequently the root cause of sleepless nights. The best mattresses are stuffed with firm yet soft natural fibres, such as cotton or

Above: *Here two lights make ideal bedside companions, creating light for reading and romance. Made from malleable metal fittings, each can be individually adjusted to the preferred angle for reading. In the morning, natural light – as much of a pick-me-up as coffee – comes flooding in.*

horsehair. 'Pocket zone sprung', or mattresses sprung with individual coils, give support and prevent 'partner roll'.

To pick a bed, always test it out first. When you're in a showroom don't be shy about kicking off your shoes and trying the bed out. The right bed to choose is one that you can sink into, but also feel supported by. Test it out by lying down on your back and wedging your hand under the small of your back. If there's a cave, the bed's too hard; if you can't slip your hand inside, the bed is too soft. If you have room, a large bed is a real luxury, for long lazy mornings in bed with loved ones. (Opting for two twin beds zipped together is not only roomy, but it also allows you to have different types of mattress for you and your partner if you wish.)

For pillows, invest in the best. The perfect pillow will support your neck and head so that they're almost in the same position relative to your body as when you're standing. Again, choose one made of the finest quality materials.

As for bedding, select something that is cosseting and comfortable. Buy untreated cotton, silk or linen – don't buy man made fibres, particularly polycottons, as these emit formaldehyde for years. For warmth, duvets, invented by the Scandinavians as the best way to contend with their cold winters, are as light as a feather. If you prefer the heavy embrace of layers of bedding, pile on pure wool blankets, or slumber under cashmere and mohair.

Induce sleep with nature's soporific colors and smells. Swathe walls in lilacs, creams and pinks or in soft neutral shades. For a somnolent scent, drop lavender on your pillow.

To create an atmosphere of calm, impose order on the bedroom. If it doubles as a dressing room, stash your clothes tidily so that it doesn't end up looking like a flea market. File your garments so that mornings run like clockwork – there's nothing worse than starting the day stumbling around to find a pair of matching socks. Free-standing or fitted wardrobes tuck clothes away, but if you have room, think about a large walk-in wardrobe. Another hideout for uncommonly used items or seasonal storage is under the bed.

A bit of organization will give you mental peace. That way your bedroom will be the perfect place to sleep, perchance to dream.

Top left: *Air circulates freely through natural fabrics, enabling the skin to 'breathe'. Bury yourself under waffle linen blankets, pure wool rugs and cotton sheets, as seen here.*

Center left: *Change your bedding to suit the season. In summer, opt for fresh stripes and cool colors, and in the winter get cosy with woollen blankets, cotton quilts and bright, cheery slippers.*

Bottom left: *Feng shui practitioners claim that the first thing you see in the morning influences your mood for the rest of the day, so wake up and smell – or just revel in – flowers. Bring happiness into your morning with bright red fresh carnations, or for calm and quiet, choose soft pink flowers.*

Opposite: *This solid bedside table has been created out of old stone wheels. A bedside table is a good place for a candle. It will create a gentle light for tired eyes, providing a welcome break from the unrelenting glare of artificial lights.*

Above: *The bed has been placed directly under a window, so the sleeper can let in fresh air and light when needed. Shutters – in a modern version of their alpine forebears – create darkness and provide insulation, while the translucent hanging softens the stark room.*

Top left: *Bedrooms don't have to be enclosed by walls on all sides. Here a bed is tucked behind a room divider. Two sculptured logs act as bedside tables.*

Above: *If your bedroom doubles as a dressing room, ensure clothes are tidily stashed away at the end of the day. Here a sleek storage wall conceals garments.*

Above: *A natural sanctuary. Designed by architect Samuel Lerch and interior designer Benjamin Thut, this beautiful bedroom resonates with Zen philosophy, exuding simplicity and restraint. A honey colored beech parquet floor, a long concrete wall with horizontal cuts concealing lighting, and a wooden storage wall make the most of natural materials. The head-high concrete dividing wall has a double sink on one side (see pages 108–9) and a Japanese style spa pool in front of it. The architectural display of flowers is the belle of the bedroom.*

living spaces

Below: *A place for talking, reading, relaxing and just living. A daybed beside a hearth provides the perfect retreat. Natural ornaments adorn shelves and the mantelpiece.* **Opposite:** *This sofa is large enough either to stretch out on or to seat company. The lilac and pink pouffes in the front provide flexible seating for extra friends. This urban oasis, with its soft, pretty pink curtains and white floors and walls, radiates calmness and serenity.*

Rooms crafted from nature's booty are effortlessly elegant – ideal for living rooms.

Strangely, the 'living room' is a modern concoction. In Victorian times, living rooms were the preserve of the poor. In aristocratic mansions, ladies took tea and gossiped in drawing rooms; gentlemen retired after dinner to billiard rooms or libraries; children and nannies were 'seen and not heard' in nurseries. Only those who were desperate to minimize fuel costs ate, sat and slept all together in one communal area.

Social change and smaller dwellings have meant that for many of us games, hobbies, children and friends all collide in one large living space. The living room is now as much a place to entertain, relax, socialize and eat as it is to sit. Sometimes it's a home office; sometimes it's a children's playground; sometimes it's a retreat. The writer Henry David Thoreau once commented, 'I have three chairs in my house: one for solitude, two for friendship, three for society.'

Each day, the demands on a living room vary like a tidal shoreline. Comfort, function and style must all be weighed up and balanced out to create a natural space that suits everybody. It's a complex equation, but by using nature to underpin all these things, aesthetics, practicality and design merge seamlessly together.

Create a congenial room by harnessing nature's most coveted elements: light, space and air. Give the living room the site in the house that receives the most sunshine, and maximize windows to let the outdoors in. Create a more spacious room if you can, possibly tearing down walls and integrating the space with the kitchen or dining room, or tacking on a glass conservatory.

Next, swathe the room's biggest canvases – the floors and walls – in materials from nature. Natural floors are hard-wearing and, unlike synthetics, they will age gracefully. Flagstones, bricks or terracotta tiles have clean, earthy looks, while polished wood or a beautiful 100 percent wool carpet or rug is warm and tactile underfoot. (For more about floors, see pages 88–93.)

Walls from natural materials make neutral backdrops and put furniture center stage. Wood, stone and leather create textural intrigue on walls,

while organic paints and papers create backgrounds that are smooth and impartial. (For more about walls, see pages 82–7.)

If the living room is to be multifunctional and multipurpose, it must be naturally adaptable. Use clever, hard-working – albeit natural – storage. The television and video recorder, for example, could be hidden in a purpose built wooden storage cabinet, inside which there could also be a hideout for videos, CDs and similar items. Or mount the television on wheels (children's toy boxes on casters are an equally good idea). Dual purpose storage, such as room dividers with shelving, also swallow up unwanted clutter, while allowing breathing space for objects that count.

Eschew pre-packaged, mass produced chairs and sofas and instead opt for daybeds, loungers, floor cushions, rocking chairs or other seating with naturally good qualities. Choose chairs made from natural fabrics, such as leather, cotton, linen or linen union. Seating is rather like a model – its dress and look can be changed with the seasons. In winter, cuddle up with lambswool cushions; in summer, clothe them in turquoise cottons or raw linens.

Select chairs that encourage good posture. A survey has revealed that an increase in back problems correlates directly with the number of hours we spend seated. Chairs, interestingly, didn't become commonplace until the sixteenth century, and even today only a third of the world sits in

them. When you sit, 30 percent more pressure is forced onto your spinal discs, so it pays to choose firm, flat surfaces that allow the weight to be transferred though your bones, rather than squashy, soft surfaces that transfer weight to muscle. Arrange chairs in a layout conducive to chat – people like to gather in circles.

Use natural light as much as possible by day. If sunlight is intrusively bright, filter it with muslin curtains or sandblasted glass. Soften window frames with curtains sewn from natural fabrics. Vary artificial lighting according to aesthetics and function. Position wall lamps, floor lights and table lamps to read by. To create atmosphere, use a mixture of halogen uplighters and downlighters to wash light over walls. And for intimacy, dim the lights and dot candles around the room.

As living rooms are public domains where we show off our favorite things, make some of yours true reflections of the things you love. The architect Christopher Alexander once mused, 'What does "beautiful" mean? It means that the thing makes me feel joyous, more rooted in the world, more whole as a person.' In nature, beauty is found in the shape of sculptural plants, pods and flowers, in beach pebbles, in conch shells. After all, mother nature is a first-rate artist and decorator.

Opposite: *Capacious seating has been arranged to facilitate conversation and sociability.*

Above left: *Nothing is quite as relaxing as flopping into the arms of a leather chair. In the corner a bamboo plant, which the Chinese believe brings wealth and prosperity, flourishes in a wooden pot.*

Above center: *A fireplace with individual flair. In this hideaway, burnt wood leaves a smudge of black soot providing a natural contrast with the pure whiteness. A door opening onto a garden blurs the boundaries between indoors and out.*

Above right: *Juxtapose soft with hard, smooth with rough, light with dark. Here a sofa is clothed in luxuriously soft sheepskin. A bamboo screen provides privacy while letting in light, and creates a textured backdrop for a Noguchi floor lamp.*

Below: *Create show-stopping natural displays with simple statements, like this spray of grasses.*

suppliers

Fire

Fireplace Store
55 Nelson Avenue
Great Kills Box 493
Staten Island, NY
10308
Tel: 718-967-5891
Email:
warmup@fireplacestore.
com
Website:
www.fireplacestore.com

Glass

Gammans Architecture Products, Inc.
(glass and glazing)
P.O. Box 2444
Newman, GA 30264
Tel: 770-254-1094
Email:
sales@gammans.com
Website:
www.gammans.com

The Glass and Glazing Federation
44 Borough High St
London
SE1 1XB
Tel: 020 7403 7177
Website:
www.ggf.org.uk

Leather

Alma Home
(leather, leather floor tiles)
12-14 Greatorex St
London
E1 5NF
Tel: 020 7377 0762
Website:
www.almahome.co.uk

Plé Designs
(leather, leather pillows)
191 Vista Lane
Yakima, WA 98908
Tel: 509-972-0235
Email:
info@pledesigns.com
Website:
www.pledesigns.com

Mattresses

Lullaby Handmade Mattresses
28 Scrubs Lane
London
NW10 6RA
Tel: 020 8968 0182
(natural mattresses)

Home Environment
216 North Henry Street
Madison, WI 53703
Tel: 877-251-4905
Email: home@home-environment.com
Website: www.home-environment.com
(organic matresses and bedding)

Metal

House of Iron
(iron furniture)
779 Fulham Rd
London
SW6 5HA
Tel: 020 7371 0436
Email:
houseofiron@talk21.com
Website:
www.houseofiron.co.uk

Iron Accents
(iron furniture)
3661 Davis Bridge Road
Gainesville, GA 30506
770-503-9018
Email:
info@ironaccents.com
Website:
www.ironaccents.com

London Metal Centre
(zinc, steel, stainless steel)
Unit 10
Titan Business Estate
Finch St
London
SE8 5QA
Tel: 020 8694 6022
Email:
sales@londonmetalcentre.co.uk
Website:
londonmetalcentre.co.uk

Nature

Glasshouse Works Items for Home, Conservatory, and Garden
Church Street
P.O. Box 97
Stewart, OH 45778
Tel: 740-662-2142
Email:plants@glasshouseworks.com
Website:
www.glasshouseworks.com

Gethsemane Gardens
(mail order)
3707 Highway 150 East
Greensboro, NC 26455
Tel: 800-599-2833
Email:
sales@gethgardens.com
Website:
www.gethgardens.com

Lucky Plants
(for bamboo)
Arotek International
Cerritos, CA
Tel: 562-921-1085
Email:
sales@luckyplants.com
Website:
www.luckyplants.com

Paint

Healthy Home.com
(natural paints)
1403-A Cleveland St.
Clearwater, FL 33755
Tel: 800-583-9523
Email:
info@healthyhome.com
Website:
www.healthyhome.com

BioShield Paints
1365 Rufina Circle
Santa Fe, NM 87505
Tel: 800-621-2591
Email:
edesignco@aol.com
Website:
www.bioshieldpaint.com

Plants and wood

The Hardwood Flooring Co. (new wood flooring)
146 West End Lane
London
NW6 1SD
Tel: 020 7328 8481

New Harbour, Inc.
(wood and cane
furniture)
1 West Street
Fall River, MA 02720
Tel: 877-678-3202
Website:
www.newharbour.com

Wicker Furniture
(mail order wicker
furniture)
Tel: 954-977-9333
Website:
www.wickerfurniture.com

LASSCO Flooring
(reclaimed wood
flooring)
41 Maltby St
London
SE1 3PA
Tel: 020 7237 4488
Email:
lasscoflo@zetnet.co.uk
Website:
www.lassco.co.uk

National Wood Flooring Association
(information and links
for wood flooring)
Website:
www.woodflooring.org

Twelve
43/44 Durant Street
London
E2 7BP
Tel: 020 7613 4878
Email:
info@twelvelimited.com
Website:
www.twelvelimited.com

Plasterwork

Hyde Park
Fine Art of Mouldings
Tel: 718-706-0504
Website:
www.hyde-park.com

Stone and tiles

Stone Age Ltd
(stone and slate)
19 Filmer Rd
London
SW6 7BU
Tel: 020 7385 7954

Fired Earth
(stone, bricks and tiles)
117-119 Fulham Rd
London
SW3 6RL
Tel: 020 7589 0489
Website:
www.firedearth.co.uk

Quint City Stone
Center
(natural tiles, stone
flooring)
7221 Northwest
Boulevard
Davenport, Iowa 52809
Tel: 319-386-2354
Email: brad@
qcstonecenter.com
Website:

www.qcstonecenter.com
Miconi Marble and TIle
(natural flooring tiles)
446 West San
Francisco Boulevard
San Rafael, CA 94901
Tel: 415-454-6844
Email:
marble@miconi.com
Website:
www.miconi.com

Textiles and fabrics

Under The Nile
(mail order organic
materials)
5792 Dichondra Place
Newark, CA 94560
Tel: 800-883-4402
Email:
utn@ix.netcom.com
Website:
www.underthenile.com

ABC Carpet and Home
(linens)
881 Broadway
New York, NY 10003
Tel: 212-473-3000
Website:
www.abchome.com

The Linen Merchant
(linens)
11 Montpelier St
London
SW7 1EX
Tel: 020 7584 3654
Website:
www.thelinenmerchant.
com

Warris Vianni & Co.
(silks, cottons, linens)
85 Goldborne Rd
London
W10 5NL
Tel: 020 8964 0069

Greenfibres (mail order
organic materials)
Freepost
LON 7805
Totnes
Devon
Tel: 01803 868 001
Email:
mail@greenfibres.com
Website:
www.greenfibres.com

Other

Eco Mall (mail order a
variety of natural and
organic products)
Website:
www.ecomall.com

Construction Resources
(great for building
advice)
16 Great Guildford St
London
SE1 0HS
Tel: 020 7450 2211
Email:
info@ecoconstruct.com
Website:
www.ecoconstruct.com

Natural Collection
(mail order natural
products for the home)
Eco House
19a Monmouth Place
Bath
BA1 2DQ
Tel: 01225 404 010
(orderline: 0840 331
3333)
Website:
www.naturalcollection.com

index

acknowledgements

The publisher would like to thank the following photographers and agencies for their kind permission to reproduce the photographs in this book:

2 Winfried Heinze/Red Cover; **4-5** Ray Main/Mainstream; **6** Guy Obijn; **7 above** Christian Sarramon; **7 above center** Mohamed Ansar/Impact; **7 below** Guy Obijn; **7 below center** John Tinning, Frank Lane Picture Agency/Corbis; **8-9** Hiroyuki Hirai(Architect: Shigeru Ban); **11 above and below** Richard Davies; **12-13** Dennis Gilber/View(Edward Cullinan Architects); **15** James Morris/Axiom; **16-17** Chris Coe/Axiom; **18** James Morris/Axiom; **19** Jan Baldwin/Narratives; **20** Michael Paul; **21** New Zealand House & Garden; **22** Edina van der Wyck/The Interior Archive(Owner: Ann Hatch); **23** Michael Paul; **24-25** Mark Luscombe Whyte/Elizabeth Whiting & Associates; **26** Guy Obijn; **27** Ray Main/ Mainstream; **28 above** Jan Verlinde; **28 below** Chris Everard/Living Etc/IPC Syndication; **29** Chris Doyle; **30** Brian Harrison/Red Cover; **31** Rodney Weidland/ Arcaid(Architect: Christina Markham); **32** Guy Obijn; **33** Simon Upton/The Interior Archive(Designer: Anthony Collett); **34 above** Guy Obijn; **34 below** Christian Sarramon; **35** Marianne Majerus; **36** Ed Reeve/The Interior Archive(Architect: Alastair Hendy); **37** Jan Baldwin/ Narratives(Architect: Pierre Lombart); **38 above** Guy Obijn; **38 below** Peter Cook/View; **39 above** Guy Obijn; **39 below** Tim Street Porter/Elizabeth Whiting & Associates; **40** Ray Main/Mainstream; **41** Guy Obijn; **42 above** Jan Verlinde; **42 below** Guy Obijn; **43** Trevor Mein/Belle/Arcaid(Architect: John Wardle); **44** Winfried Heinze/Red Cover; **46-47** Martyn Thompson/ESP (Architect: Alastair Hendy); **48** Winfried Heinze/Red Cover; **49** Guy Obijn; **50 left** Solvi Dos Santos; **50 right** Winfried Heinze/Red Cover; **50 center**

Ray Main/ Mainstream (Architects: McDowel & Benedetti); **51** Peter Cook/ View; **52** Piere Peres/La Casa de Marie Claire(Stylist: Ino Coll); **53** Ray Main/ Mainstream; **54 above left** Jan Verlinde (Architect: Stephanie Laperre); **54 above right** Verne Fotografie; **54 below** Jan Verlinde; **55-56** Solvi Dos Santos; **57** Bieke Claessens; **58** Verity Welstead/Red Cover; **59 above** Verne Fotografie; **59 below left** Deidi von Schaewen (Chateau Chambellan, library designed by Garouste and Bonetti); **59 below right** Andrew Wood/The Interior Archive(Architect: Spencer Fung); **60** Doreen Dierckx; **61** Guy Obijn(Architect: Carlo Seminck); **62 left** Peter Cook/View; **62 right** Jan Verlinde; **62 center** Christian Sarramon; **63 above left and above right** Guy Obijn (Architect: Carlo Seminck); **63 below** Simon Upton/The Interior Archive(Designer: Andrea Truglio); **64** Jan Verlinde; **65** Guy Obijn; **66 left** Ray Main/Mainstream; **66 right** Jim Hensley; **67** Nick Pope; **68 left** Guy Obijn; **68 right** and **69** Solvi Dos Santos; **70** M-P Morel/Marie Claire Maison(Stylist D. Rozensztroch); **71** Harvey Male/Impact; **72** Peter Dixon/Narratives; **73 above** N.Tosi/Marie Claire Maison (Stylist: C.Ardouin); **73 below left** and **below right** Solvi Dos Santos; **74-75** Jacqui Hurst; **76** Nick Huggins/Houses and Interiors; **77 above** Chris Coe/Axiom; **77 below** C. Bradley/Axiom; **78 above** Jenny Acheson/ Axiom; **78 below** Verne Fotografie (Architects: Bataille & Ibens); **79 above** Simon Brown/The Interior Archive(Designer: Margaret Howell); **79 center** Ed Reeve/ The Interior Archive; **79 below left** Alexander van Berge; **79 below right** Polly Wreford/ Narratives; **80-81** N. Tosi/ Marie Claire Maison (Stylist: C. Ardouin); **82** Alexander van Berge; **83** Christian Sarramon; **84** Guy Obijn (Architect:

Vincent van Duysen); **85** Verne Fotografie; **86 above** Bieke Claessens (Stylist: Sofia Bostyn); **86 below** Giorgio Possenti/Vega MG; **87** Guy Obijn; **88** Tom Stewart/Alma; **89** Alexander van Berge; **90** A.F. Pelissier/Maison Madame Figaro; **91** Ricardo Labougle; **92 left** Jan Verlinde; **92 right** Jan Verlinde (Interior designer: Jan Wals); **93** Ray Main/ Mainstream; **94** Bieke Claessens; **95** Alexander van Berge; **96** Verity Welstead/ Red Cover; **97 above** Jan Verlinde; **97 below left** Guy Obijn; **97 below right** Verne Fotografie; **98** Jan Verlinde(Architects: Bataille & Ibens); **99** Michael Paul (Architect: Alastair Hendy); **100 above** Ariadne Ahrens/Twins(Stylist: Margret Ahrens-Dulfer); **100 above right** Christian Sarramon; **100 below** Ray Main/Mainstream; **101** N.Tosi/Marie Claire Maison(C.Ardouin); **102** Verne Fotografie; **103** Luke White/ The Interior Archive(Owner: Hannah Woodhouse; **104** Luke White/The Interior Archive (Owner: Shaw); **105** Verne Fotografie; **106 above** Ray Main/Mainstream; **106 below** Guy Obijn; **107** Jan Verlinde; **108-109** Bruno Helbling; **110** Ray Main/ Mainstream; **111** Eric Morin; **112** Guy Obijn; **113** Jan Verlinde (Architect: Alex van de Walle); **114 above** Wayne Vincent/The Interior Archive; **114 below left** Edina van der Wyck/The Interior Archive (Owner: Willy); **114 below right** Verne Fotografie (Architect: Stuart Parr); **115 above left** Guy Obijn; **115 above center** Simon Brown/The Interior Archive (Designer: Margaret Howell); **115 above right** Ray Main/ Mainstream; **115 below** Doreen Dierckx; **116** Ray Main/Mainstream(Architects: McDowel & Benedetti); **117 above** Jake Fitzjones/Houses and Interiors; **117 below** Ray Main/Mainstream; **118** Jim Hensley; **119** Ken Hayden/ Red Cover(Architect: John Pawson); **120** Andreas von Einsiedel/Red Cover; **121** A. Bailhache/Marie Claire

Maison (Stylist: A.M. Comte); **122 above left** Winfried Heinze/Red Cover; **122 above right** Jan Baldwin/Narratives; **122 below left** Ray Main/ Mainstream(Designer: Andrew Martin); **122 below right** Ray Main/Mainstream; **123** Son Lindman; **124 above left** Bieke Claessens (Stylist: Sofia Bostyn); **124 above right** and **below** Guy Obijn; **125** Winfried Heinze/Red Cover; **126** Polly Wreford/ Narratives; **127** Ray Main/Mainstream; **128 above** N. Bruant/Maison Madame Figaro; **128 below** Graham Atkins hughes/Living Etc/IPC magazines; **129** Guy Obijn (Architect: Vincent van Duysen); **130 above** Graham Atkins-Hughes/Red Cover; **130 center** Graham Atkins-Hughes/Red Cover; **130 below** Polly Wreford/ Narratives; **131** A. F. Pelissier/Maison Madame Figaro; **132 above left** Bieke Claessens; **132 above right** M.P. Morel/Marie Claire Maison(Stylist: C. Puech); **132 below** Bieke Claessens; **133** Bruno Helbling; **134** Winfried Heinze/Red Cover; **135** Ray Main/Mainstream; **136** Ken Hayden/Red Cover; **137 above left** Andrew Wood/The Interior Archive (Designer: Leonie Lee); **137 above center** Paul Ryan/ International Interiors (Designer: Jacqueline Morabito); **137 above right** Inside/The Interior Archive (Magazine: House & Leisure/Dook); **137 below** Jan Verlinde

The publisher and authors would also like to thank Cale Associates (020 8960 9027) for the loan of the lounger (designed by Bruno Mathon) in the front jacket photograph and Story (020 7377 0313) for the bowls in the back jacket photograph.

Every effort has been made to trace the copyright holders and we apologize in advance for any unintentional omission and would be pleased to insert the appropriate acknowledgement in any subsequent edition.